Your
First Year
of Marriage

Curtis Pesmen

A Fireside Book

PUBLISHED BY SIMON & SCHUSTER

NEW YORK   LONDON   TORONTO   SYDNEY   TOKYO   SINGAPORE

F

FIRESIDE
Rockefeller Center
1230 Avenue of the Americas
New York, NY 10020

Manufactured in the United States of America

10   9   8   7   6   5   4   3   2   1

Library of Congress Cataloging-in-Publication Data
Pesmen, Curtis.
   Your first year of marriage / Curtis Pesmen.
      p.   cm.
   includes index.
   1. Marriage.   2. Married people.   I. Title.
HQ734.P49   1995   95-17631
306.81—dc20   CIP
Design by Crowded House

ISBN 0-684-80246-5

For Paula

Acknowledgments

Since this book is about couples, there are a couple of people I'd like to thank first: Terry Real, of the Family Institute of Cambridge, Massachusetts, and Nancy Taylor, of Alencon Bridal Salon, Mill Valley, California. Both helped out in big ways of which probably not aware.

To the dozens of brides, grooms and not-so-newly wed who sat for interviews and spoke your minds, I thank you and remind you that without your help and insights, this book wouldn't have been possible. (To Helen and Orlo, my octogenarian newlyweds, thanks for reminding me that romance is as important in one's eighties as it is in one's twenties.)

I'd also like to acknowledge Courtney Barry, Barbara Brabec, Gregg Goldstein, Karlin McCarthy, Linda Simon, Rose Stremel-Helion, and Jennifer Wolff for their expert research and reporting.

Many other friends and colleagues offered encouragement and valued assistance along the way, including Millie Martini Bratten of BRIDE'S, Philippa Brophy, Bob Condor, Nancy Duffy, Cindy Gitter, Geoff Hansen, Peter Korn, Kara Leverte, Renny Logan, Julie Merberg, Todd Neal, Alexandra Penney at SELF, Scott Raab, Mark and Jennifer Radcliffe, Michael Schrage, and Mark Zwonitzer.

Closer to home, I give heartfelt thanks to Laura and Steve Sattler, Beth and Howard Preis, and my mother and father, Sandra and Harold Pesmen (now in their forty-third year of marriage), for their suggestions and support.

Long before this book took shape, an amazing woman convinced me that there was a place and a need for it and that I should be its author. That woman, Paula DuPré, eventually became Paula DuPré Pesmen. For her insights, for her help in pre- and postproduction, I am so thankful. For teaching me, always, about love, I am eternally grateful.

Contents

Foreword

If it weren't for sex, if it weren't for secrets, and if it weren't for secrets about sex, this book about marriage would not have been written.

In the early 1990s, I interviewed dozens of women for my book *What She Wants: A Man's Guide to Women,* and many of those interviews were with strangers. Early on, I told these women that I was writing a book for men—to help them deal with women—and that I hoped my interviewees could help me. They did. And what struck me halfway through my research was how many of these women told me things about their bodies and their sex lives that they did not or could not tell their boyfriends or husbands.

I could understand it, perhaps, if it were a new relationship. Or if someone had been dating two or three guys at a time. But as a single man in the midst of a long-term relationship, I could not make sense of wives keeping such significant secrets from their husbands.

The fact was, they were telling a near stranger—me—things they *wished* they could tell the men they had married ostensibly forever. But somehow they couldn't bring themselves to tell their husbands to slow down, to caress them more, to go easier on their sensitive parts, because they were afraid of hurting their feelings. Some of these women were recently married, while others had been married three or four years. All of them had things to say but didn't know quite how to say them to the men they slept with every night.

Afraid of hurting their husbands' feelings?

That stayed with me, and it led me to write the book you are now reading. If couples could get locked into such potentially damaging patterns so early in a marriage, I wondered, when did the patterns begin? During courtship or engagement? More likely they began in the first year of marriage, because that was when the ultimate sharing of lives was supposed to have begun. And for some reason it didn't.

 *had al-*

ways felt that

once you were

married, you had

no more secrets.

As someone who remained single through his twenties and early thirties, and who was raised by two parents who have been married more than forty years, I had always felt that once you were married, you had no more secrets. Then I did some reading on the subject, interviewed a number of couples and marital therapists, and found out otherwise.

A lot of married couples do keep secrets from each other—even happily married couples—but it turns out the happy couples tend not to hide their sexual wants and needs. Instead they may keep a secret or two about a fantasy, a former lover, or even about a friend, and as you'll see, there's nothing necessarily wrong with that.

But as for sexual and marital secrets, what I learned long ago still holds: a husband and wife need to tell each other what they want, even if they can't quite say it aloud. Fortunately, there are other ways to say such things, as you'll hear from the newlyweds interviewed in these pages.

There will be other secrets gleaned from the seventy-five couples interviewed here—about closet eating habits (Chapter 3), secret money stashes (Chapter 7), and ex-lovers (Chapter 4), to name a few. But the first year of marriage, I found out, is so much more than secrets. I should know: when I began this book I was single. As I write this, I am in my ninth month of marriage and still giddy. I know it's early—everybody keeps reminding my wife Paula and me about that. But it is also a year that has changed who we are. And that's no secret.

CHAPTER I

The

Wedding

Day

THE FIRST DAY OF THE FIRST YEAR

*nce upon a time there was a lovely bride
and a handsome groom who had a
perfect storybook wedding . . .*

—advertisement for Walt Disney World resort
in *Modern Bride* magazine

nce upon a roller coaster, Leslie Fratkin and David Lindsay had a storybook wedding far, far away from the world of Disney. Against their parents' early wishes, on a Saturday in June, Leslie and David, two creative types from Greenwich Village in New York City, got married on the historic Cyclone roller coaster on Coney Island in a ceremony that was described as unforgettable, even if it wasn't perfect. When they said, "I do," they really did.

There was sunshine, wind, cotton candy, saltwater taffy, and a couple of television news crews. There were forty-two guests, all of whom had received two souvenir ADMIT ONE carnival-ride ticket stubs along with their invitations. But more memorable was the wedding itself. It was staged on a ride that symbolized marriage pretty well, with its ups and downs, fears, laughs, even tears— and, for good measure, a clackety climb followed by a plunging rush of emotion that sent bride and groom screaming around the vintage track. Leslie and David made sure their wedding day was as memorable as it was unorthodox.

As for their relationship roles, Leslie explained, "I'm the glitter, and he's the glue."

There was other glitter, too. It turned out that CNN broadcast the news of the marriage around the world on cable TV. Nearer to home, the New York *Daily News* ran a photo of the nuptials, while two local television channels filed their own reports. And Leslie, a freelance photographer and picture editor, took three rolls of photos of her own during the ceremony, which three months later, on a lark, she tried to peddle to *BRIDE'S* magazine. She succeeded; on that day her glitter stuck like glue. In the following January issue, on page 22, Leslie and David's wedding was featured as a ceremony worthy of special mention in the largest bridal magazine in the United States.

But perfect? No, it wasn't. Maybe "storybook" would be quite enough for Leslie and Dave, a writer of stories himself, considering all the mentions they got in the media. Besides, the Coney Island site cost $10,000 less than a fantasy affair at Disney World.

"We were pronounced man and wife on the tracks of the Cyclone."

As you know by now or are soon to find out, when it comes to the first year of marriage, the wedding is barely the beginning. Call it Day Zero if you want to get technical, but it is also the day that becomes Day One—the first day of a couple's first year of husband-and-wife, of married life, of love till death you won't part. And the frustrating thing to remember is that love alone isn't enough to carry a couple seamlessly through the often turbulent first day and first year.

"We were pronounced man and wife on the tracks of the Cyclone," Dave said proudly, ten months after the event. "But we had to stop and wait for Channel 2 news to arrive."

Leslie, who doesn't like to wait for anything, would

No matter how big or small your wedding day turns out to be, there are some things you will always remember and a few things you would rather forget.

have preferred to barrel on ahead, to get the wedding show *moving*. But Dave, the patient one who had been engaged twice before yet had never married, didn't mind waiting another few minutes.

In retrospect, maybe the mini-standoff shouldn't have been surprising. "Even though we are aware of personal differences," say Melvyn Kinder, Ph.D., and Connell Cowan, Ph.D., authors of *Husbands and Wives*, "they seem insignificant in those wonderfully accepting early stages of marriage."

Especially in the *earliest* stage of marriage. No matter how big or small your wedding day turns out to be, there are some things you will always remember and a few things you would rather forget. Then there are the things you wish you had done differently. While the big bridal magazines are chock-full of ads for Galina gowns and Noritake china and lists of things to do to make a wedding run smoothly, they are deficient in one important respect: they don't take a lot of time to tell their readers how to savor the emotional highs of one of the most emotional days of a bride and groom's life. For that advice, it helps to talk with those who've recently been through it.

Katie, twenty-eight, for one, a newlywed from Tulsa, Oklahoma, told me she felt different from many of her married female friends because, when it came time to sweat the details, she uncharacteristically ended up soothing the nerves of her groom-to-be. "I told Mike throughout everything," she said, "'It's inevitable that some things are going to go wrong. So the thing that we have to remember is that, as long as you and I are there—and we get married—that's all that matters. You know what I mean?'" She also told him, knowing how much he likes to keep things under control, "You're going to have problems with the relatives and the vibes—and you know, what if the flowers aren't right or something? You can sit there and you can worry about it; then you'll dwell on it; and that's going to wreck the day, you know? But as long as we're both there and we make it through the honeymoon, that's what matters."

Cheryl and Kevin Mitchell of Boston, on the other hand, *wanted* to believe in fairy tales on their wedding day. They called up the folks at Disney World and signed up for a package that included the wedding ceremony, a reception for 125 people, and a honeymoon at the Disney Yacht and Beach Club in Orlando, Florida. Kevin, a general manager of a popular downtown restaurant, even sprang for the ultimate in wedding accessories for his bride: she arrived at the ceremony in a Cinderella glass pumpkin coach, drawn by a team of horses, heigh-ho, heigh-ho (the coach cost an extra $1,000).

"Cheryl's been to Disney World every year since it opened," Kevin explained. "She turned me on to Disney." For them, the details of the Big Day—the script—meant a lot.

For my fiancée, Paula, and me, to take another example, tradition meant more than glitter. She and I even agreed, three months into our engagement, that we didn't want to have our wedding videotaped. This ran contrary to the wedding trends we'd read about and contrary to the advice of many of our friends, including my best man, who told me flat out that he thought we were making a mistake. (After all, he and his bride had had *their* ceremony videotaped professionally a couple of years before.) It wasn't that we viewed videography as crass or evil, or that we found the cost excessive, or even that we were hopelessly old-fashioned. But we had both been to a number of weddings over the past five years at which the videographer or camera had seemed intrusive. Sometimes the camera's lights were too bright, or the assistant or the power cord got in the way—and the feeling of intimacy during the ceremony seemed to suffer.

We—a couple who had lived together for four months before our marriage and who had rented fewer than four videos from the corner store together during that time—just didn't feel we needed a videotaped record of our marriage. Or so we thought. Less than five weeks after we were married, we found ourselves one night talking about the wedding and agreeing that it would have been nice to have taped "at least the ceremony part, maybe just twenty minutes." We also agreed—after the fact—that it would have been nice at least to have had the ceremony audiotaped on cassette for a kind of oral-history keepsake. Two of our other friends, who had married in the Neolithic Pre-camcorder era of the 1970s, had done that and were glad they had. They still listen to their scratchy audio vows every once in a while; not just on their anniversary.

In any event, partly to compensate for our ambivalence or guilt, we ended up ordering dozens more overpriced three-by-five reprints (at $7.00 apiece!) from our photographer than we would have otherwise. We were lucky, too, that one of Paula's cousins was a photographer: he shot five rolls of black-and-white film that night as a wedding present without our having asked him to or having directed him in any way. He had heard (rightly) that we had been thinking of having a black-and-white photographer, in addition to the portrait photographer, in order to capture the informal moments of the wedding—but we had never gone ahead with the idea. As it turned out, my new cousin-in-law caught dozens of behind-the-scenes candid moments that a videographer might have missed. These, we figure, will forever serve as our own documentary of Day One—even if they never see the light of a VCR or TV. You could call it rationalization. We called it a lucky break.

Vows for the Record

Lois Smith Brady, thirty-six, has seen more than her share of wedding-day videos, many of which she wishes she could have fast-forwarded. An unlicensed expert on the first day of the first year of marriage, Brady is neither a minister nor a wedding consultant: she watches weddings for a living. She then writes about the more interesting and entertaining ones in a column called "Vows" in the Sunday edition of the *New York Times.* Brady has had this odd job for the newspaper of record since 1992, and prior to that she wrote a similarly quirky column about marriages for *7 Days*, a now-defunct New York City magazine. One spring evening, in a cheerful but barren Manhattan café, Brady, who herself has been married six years, talked about the ceremonies she observes on weekends and writes about Monday after Monday after Monday.

"They're kind of like movies," she said. "You always remember the great ones.

"This Saturday I'm doing two weddings," Brady said, "one in the afternoon and one at night." This seemed to please her because, as I later found out, by doing two in one day she could write about both over the next few days and take the next weekend off. (The *Times* runs only one "Vows" report each week.) When I asked her whether there were any secret ways she knew of to predict, simply by studying the ceremony, whether a marriage would last, she said, "I go partly by the attitude of the guests, because that's whom I talk to more than anyone else. They're so much more opinionated than you'd think. Friends are either so sugary—or totally snide. A lot of times people just say positive things because that's what they're supposed to say."

Brady is not so much cynical about weddings as she is honest. Her scissor-sharp truths are based on what she often sees on days that are supposed to be full of nothing but romp and circumstance. If she attends a real loser of a wedding, she'll still write about it, but her editors will usually hold the story.

"I talk with the bride and groom a lot beforehand, usually for the first time about a month before," Brady said. This enables her to sketch the characters in her stories well before the big event. And on occasion a bride or groom will let slip with lines of dialogue that telegraph what's to come on the wedding day. "One bride I talked with recently was *so* much in love," Brady said. "She said, *'I just can't believe that this incredibly smart, funny guy is marrying ME!'*" It was no faux low-self-esteem put-down; it was an excitable preview of a promising first year.

If Looks Could Thrill

"I look to see if a couple have an amazement in how they look at each other," Brady told me. "Sometimes they are truly shocked! That's what I think people mean when they say the bride is 'in an altered state.' . . . It's that they cannot believe their phenomenal luck.

"Immediately after they say their vows is a wild time to see a couple together . . . in their first few minutes." One reliable guide Brady always looks for is the way a couple looks at each other during their vows. "It is so re*veal*ing," she said. In describing one couple whom she had written about some months ago and who had broken up six months later, she said, "The guy, I remember, never looked at her at all. He was looking at all of his friends, with a little smirk, and she was staring at him. He was avoiding her eyes."

To be sure, *The Look* means a lot, but the vows and the look together mean a whole lot more. Just ask Jeanie, thirty-two, a newlywed from northern California, who married her husband in a secular ceremony that included 120 guests and vows they had written—and rewritten—themselves. "When we were saying our vows I felt we were speaking to each other, not that we were in front of other people," she said. "My preconceived notion was that we would be *performing*. But as it turned out, it was really emotional—I had a lump in my throat. Some tears, too, because I felt what we said was coming out of our hearts.

"*Okay, this is it. We've done it.*"

"I remember, immediately after the kiss," Jeanie said, "we held hands and gave each other a few squeezes, as if to say, 'Okay, this is it. We've *done* it.' Then, when we turned around and looked at our friends and family for the first time, it finally occurred to me that all these people had really been listening to what we were saying.

"And that's when I heard this clapping, and everybody started standing up and smiling," she continued. "It wasn't just applause; they were clapping really vigorously. At the time it felt so personal. And when I saw their reactions I said, 'God, *they* were as into it as we were!'" (Despite the nondenominational ceremony, Jeanie seems to have included God in the wedding after all.)

When it comes to vows, she, like thousands of modern brides, believes it is really worth it for a couple to make the time to write their own, or at least to have input about what a minister or judge will say. While Jeanie's vows focused on the meaning of marriage, her groom's contained his promises and pledges to her. They didn't match or necessarily mirror each other, and that turned out fine.

"What we ended up doing," she said, "is talking heart to heart. We may have changed the words some from when we first sat down to try to write them, but they ended up being close to what we wrote the first night. We only did two practice runs the week of the wedding, and I cried. Then I stopped and put them [the vows] away. They meant more to us that way, because we didn't become numb by hearing them over and over. They didn't sound rehearsed or feel too rehearsed. We had them mounted on cards, and the words were more ours than lines from a poem, or verse. Our cards were a cue to remind us of the direction we wanted to take. But there were no rules."

"Obedience is largely out. Cherishing is in."

Actually, there are a couple of rules to consider when writing your own vows in these modern times, if you heed the words of Jennifer Rogers, author of *Tried and Trousseau: The Bride Guide.* "To begin with," she says, "it's important to get clear what's being agreed upon. Obedience is largely out. Cherishing is in. The rest is negotiable." The rest *is* negotiable.

As for Leslie Fratkin and Dave Lindsay, they liked their vows so much they said them twice: once during the small ceremony on the roller coaster, the second time at their reception, with more relatives and friends, in a friend's loft on Renwick Street in lower Manhattan later the same day. During the second ceremony, which included a heartfelt mention of Dave's father, who had recently died, the minister said, "In their nearly two years together, David and Leslie have already been through good times and difficult times, and they have learned much about the beginnings of a lifelong relationship. Their marriage, then, honors that beginning. It also serves as a gate through which they now pass."

Although she originally had intended to, Lois Smith Brady didn't end up covering Leslie and Dave's wedding for her newspaper column. At the last minute, Brady was reassigned to the wedding of then New York governor Mario Cuomo's daughter. In a battle for news coverage between the newly wedded cute or the powerful in the largest city in the country, this round clearly went to Super Mario's daughter.

"One other thing I've noticed," said Brady, who, incidentally, voted for the bride's father, "is, depending on how long a couple has held their stare during the ceremony, they've made me cry"—at which point Brady turned her eyes away from mine toward the center of the café. "There has to be some incredible depth there. It makes it all so unbelievable. I always look at how they look at each other.

"It's just indicative of a bond. You can tell. It's like holding hands, but multiplied a hundred times. It, to me, is the ultimate expression of their union, when their eyes lock. Because eyes just don't *lock,* you know?"

In related fashion, during the ceremonies she covers, Brady pays mind to how each couple handles nerves. At one recent wedding she attended, the groom was forty-five or so; the bride, forty-two. He was handsome, tall, and shaky; she was gregarious, not short, and funny. Early on, Brady noticed that the bride took her groom's hand into her left hand and started rubbing it lightly, again and again, with the fingers of her right hand. He had been a longtime bachelor and was apparently very stiff. The interesting thing was, the bride had told Brady before the ceremony that she *thought* he was going to be nervous. So she was prepared. Ready to take care of him. On their first day of marriage!

At a very different wedding covered by the *Times* some months earlier, between two people in their twenties who had met at an aerobics studio, the groom was a TV-production type from Australia, the bride was an actress, and he broke down and cried during the ceremony. Not exactly on cue. A couple of weeks afterward, one of the guests told Brady flat out: "After watching that ceremony, I broke up with my girlfriend of three years." This wedding guest could tell that the love between these two people was nothing like his and his girlfriend's, and ultimately he said to himself: "I want to hold out for *that*."

"When I wrote about that wedding," Brady said, "I remember saying, 'Aussies are known for wrestling alligators, not weeping.' I also remember that he had lost his parents, that he and his bride were both in their late twenties, and it was very moving. She immediately thought of comforting him."

At the Mitchells' Disney World wedding, by contrast, neither Cheryl nor Kevin worried too much about comforting each other. They had Cheryl's four-year-old daughter from her first marriage to think about. As it turned out, they needn't have worried: a fairy-tale setting works just fine in soothing the qualms of a skeptical child about to take on a new mom or dad. Even so, the parameters of their marriage didn't take long to become established: it seemed as if not just two, but all three of them got married that day. When I talked with them seven months after the wedding, Cheryl and Kevin delighted in telling the details of how their daughter was included in the vows and how you couldn't exactly get married in the shadow of Mickey and Minnie Mouse *without* looking through the eyes of a child. (On the other hand, when I watched a Disney wedding one spring day at one of the famed resorts, I couldn't help but notice that the guests seemed to be preoccupied with the life-sized characters Mickey and Minnie. Too many of them worried about posing with the formally attired human-sized mice instead of talking with and taking pictures of the real stars of the day—the bride and groom.)

The First Kiss

When it comes to performance of a more traditional kind—a couple's first kiss—many of the wedding sages with whom I spoke (including photographers and caterers) said, somewhat surprisingly, that this act was often more symbolic than emotional. I found this odd at first, for two reasons. First, a personal one: my bride and I happened to have had a wonderful first kiss, full-mouthed and warm, while we stood beneath spotlights and beside a huge spiral staircase in the Chicago Historical Society. I remember holding Paula's head in my right hand in a way I never had before, and yet it felt as if we had kissed this way before. Second: it seems cold to consider a first kiss as merely symbolic. After all, this is not just the first kiss of a couple's married life: it is the first sexual activity of a newlywed couple's life. And even if they are nervous, you'd think they would want to freeze the moment and get a little boost of strength from each other. You'd think . . .

"I really, honestly believe it isn't that big a deal," Brady told me. "Sometimes you see people give these amazing kisses, but when you think about it, they may not be that amazing. Your eyes are closed, and it's a bigger, less personal moment [as if it's acting]. So I never judge a couple by the kiss. Some are really tight—they hold each other tightly—others are just a peck. And others, I think, are uncomfortable.

"The kiss doesn't say anything. To me.

"Some brides may remember it as the first kiss of their married life, but some may just remember it as the beginning of the next stage of the wedding." By then, the music may have already started playing.

"Maybe the first kiss is a personal thing," Brady said, "but I can't even remember how it went at my wedding (five and a half years ago). I don't have a video, either. All I remember was that our kiss was very, *fwpwah!*— just a pucker. And I always wonder if couples French-kiss. . . . It's an amazing kiss, but from my point of view it's not a telling thing."

Helen, a twenty-nine-year-old newlywed from Philadelphia, who married a Frenchman, had a similarly plebian point of view: her first French kiss of married life was less than enthralling. "In France," she told me, "the typical Catholic wedding doesn't have a 'You may now kiss the bride' part. So Jean-Cristophe [her groom] wasn't prepared to really kiss me in front of everyone at the wedding. We really didn't work on it during the rehearsal. So it was a wimpy peck, and I said, '*Wait* a minute!'"

In contrast, back on the Cyclone, Leslie and Dave remember fondly and proudly their storybook smooch upon becoming husband and wife. "It was great," Leslie said of the kiss that she got on the urban shore of the Atlantic, where it's not safe to stroll the boardwalk at night. "It still somehow seemed private."

Setting Up the Setting

Like Leslie and Dave, the couples today who seem most proud of their weddings generally are those who had a hand in creating the look and feel of the ceremony. More than ever—and not just because of increased interfaith and second and third marriages—couples are choosing to be married outside of churches and temples, in restaurants, private clubs, city halls, spruced-up barns, beaches, Las Vegas chapels, Caribbean resorts, restored urban homes, or suburban manors. "If the setting is *connected* to a couple, it means more," Brady related. "There is one couple getting married this June who are having the ceremony in the Boathouse in Central Park, because it turns out they met in Central Park while running. Maybe the Central Park thing is overdone, but this kind of wedding adds resonance if the location fits into the couple's story."

There was a very different sort of couple I met with, more traditionally minded, who both grew up in Chicago but now live in the Washington, D.C., suburbs. They knew right away they had found the *right* Chicago church in which to be married. It was Old St. Patrick's on Adams Street, which despite its age was enjoying a revival of sorts in its congregation. But first this couple had to solve a problem—religion. The groom, unlike the bride, wasn't Catholic. And she had her heart set on the place, not because of its architecture, nor for the fact that the St. Patrick's Day celebration in Chicago begins every year outside the church's front door. It was because of the lofty reputation of the Reverend Jack Wall, who had known the bride's family. After the groom went ahead and converted to Catholicism (he felt that he wanted to give his bride something meaningful in return, because she would be moving away from her parents and friends to his home out East), Father Wall offered the couple advice that made them both feel like longtime members of the congregation.

He told them, during their church-sponsored pre-

Cana (marital) workshops, that they were going to face
times when they would "get swept away with the wedding planning, or by this or that, and that you simply
won't be thinking about why you will be in church that
day." And as Michelle, the bride, remembers it, he
added, "I know that will be the case, but I always want
you to remember, soulfully, what this day means. And
whenever you think about something that stresses you
about the ceremony—stop and tie that down to something in your soul about the day itself."

"He meant," she explained, "that this may be bad
stress or this is distracting to me, but it is distracting me
from the soulful reason that I am here today. Or that
I'm going to be there that day with my husband."

No matter what your religion, the setting of the wedding can be profoundly influenced by these kinds of
questions. As Thomas Moore writes in the recent best-
seller *Soul Mates*: "Some marriages characteristically
ask for distance, others for closeness; some apparently
want to be brief, some lifelong. . . . Some accent emotions of bliss, some pain. Some marriages prefer senti-
mentality, others like pragmatism." It seems that Moore
could just as easily have been writing these words
about weddings as about marriages. For in a way he is
writing as much about personalities as the institution of
marriage itself.

"I went to one wedding," Lois Smith Brady told me,
"that was held in this funky little beach house—it was
Hopperesque, with the front door slamming behind
you and all—where the couple had spent all these
summers hanging out and reading paperback books.
You could imagine the lobster dinners they had on the
porch. They had a hundred and twenty-five people
packed like a phone booth into this little house, with a
band playing in the corner, and you could feel the intimacy of their lives. There was also this big rock near

the front door, where they'd throw their swimsuits to dry because it got real hot in the sun. You could feel it, almost like there was sand on the floor." This couple met in boarding school, it turned out, and they could have afforded a wedding almost anywhere. Yet they fell in love *there,* and that's probably why it was as charming a place for a wedding as it was. "How does the saying go?" Brady said. "God lives in the details? God is *in* the details. There's truth to that."

In decorating the house, they took dozens of shells that they'd found together, Brady said, "and made place cards with shells glued to them. Each table was named with one of their 'landmarks' from the town: their favorite beach; the Carousel, the shop where they'd get ice cream; that kind of thing. It was like we were invited on a tour through their relationship. It was amazing."

From Day Zero to Day One

When John Gregory Dunne, the screenwriter and author of *True Confessions* and *Harp*, married Joan Didion, the screenwriter and author of *Slouching Towards Bethlehem* and *The White Album,* some thirty years ago in a little mission church in San Juan Bautista, California, they weren't big famous Hollywood writers. Yet. And so they wouldn't have begun to think of a mega-wedding weekend bash like the reported $400,000 affair that Geena Davis and her groom, director Renny Harlin, threw in September of 1993, when they all but took over Sonoma County, California, and entertained the likes of Sylvester Stallone and his entourage.

No, Dunne and Didion were merely on their way, back then. A quaint mission church would do. As Dunne remembered his first day of his first year of marriage, in the pages of *Esquire* in 1990: "As we walked down the aisle," he wrote, "we promised each other that we could get out of this next week and not wait until death did us part. That promise was the bedrock of the marriage."

As writers, Dunne and Didion are forever careful with their words, even if they weren't on their wedding day. I once worked with Mr. Dunne by phone, and over a course of weeks I got to know the tenor of his words a little bit, both spoken and written. It seemed to me that sometimes he didn't always mean what he wrote, but he wrote it anyway and hoped that you got it. He was confident that way.

So I'm guessing that, when he told his bride in the church that day that they could "get out of" their marriage "next week," he was winking at her with words and she winked back. What they really meant, I'd venture to say, is that they would give each other room and time to maneuver through the scraggly patches of their love. It is sage advice to have come from such a cynical couple in the cynical decade of the Sixties. Maybe it worked because it was honest, even as it wasn't: more than anything, Dunne and Didion didn't try to make too much of their wedding day. They treated it with a modicum of respect, stopping short of awe and leaving room for it to breathe, to sink in. Which is what a wedding wants, even if its star participants, both bride and groom, don't yet know it.

Looking back much more recently, Katie Smith, the twenty-eight-year-old newlywed and fitness instructor from Tulsa, told me that back in the late 1980s she had vastly different thoughts about her (potential) wedding day, depending on how involved she was in a particular relationship at a given time. "Maybe it's too analytical," she said, "but I remember before being engaged, like, *all* I thought about was the wedding, the cere-

mony, the party. And not about the marriage. And
when I actually stopped to think about that, I went,
'Oh, shit. I can't do this! I don't know if I love this person.'" When she got to really know Mike, her eventual
husband, however, these doubts existed no longer.
That's not to say there were no doubts; it's just that
they were different. Once she finally felt secure about
her biggest decision—the groom—the doubts shifted to
the area of family pressures and the expectations of
others related to the wedding.

Which, it turned out, were easier for Katie to handle
because they were so much smaller in comparison. The
question of whether there was enough love in her
heart to marry was moot. On her wedding day, the storybook part was evident on her face, as her husband
later described it. And I believe him, because it was still
quite evident on both their faces six months later,
when I visited their apartment in Tulsa. They are the
kind of couple who can make a party out of a couple
of cans of Diet Coke, a few photos, and a handful of
memories. I've seen them do it.

So now we know. On the first day of marriage there
is *the setting,* there are *the vows,* there is *the kiss,* and
there is *the look.* All this happens, the statistics tell us,
2.3 million times each year in the United States. We also
know these are the big four themes of the day couples
can indeed wrest control of, no matter what they might
have heard about weddings spinning out of control.
And in so doing they can start their first year off under
their own power, on their own course, despite having
been drained of energy and emotion in those last few
weeks before becoming, well, one.

CHAPTER 2

The Truth

About

Honeymoons

Do not refuse one another except perhaps by agreement for a season.

—1 Corinthians 7

nce the pressures of planning and performing at your wedding are over, you'd think you'd have it easy. You *should* have it easy. After all, the celebration went off with only one or two hitches; the dress has been sent to the cleaner for cleaning-boxing-sealing; the tuxes have gone back to the rental store (minus a few cuff links); and now it's time for the two of you to celebrate. Alone. And yet, as soon as your honeymoon—your escape—begins, another pressure inevitably arises. Which many couples find surprising.

Maybe they shouldn't. For the conventional wisdom goes something like the following:

> *On this, the first day after your wedding, you MUST now have a WONDERFUL time on your honeymoon, and you MUST have GREAT sex, because this is the most BLISS-FUL time of your life—of your brand new MARRIAGE—and if you don't have INTERCOURSE at least three times each day for seven or ten days, you are in grave DAN-GER of suffering a loss of confidence in the UNION you have just made under the watchful eyes of your fam-*

*ily, friends, in-laws, and, quite possibly, the Lord. Or
so it is said.*

You think that's not a bit stressful for two spanking
new newlyweds? I asked a Chicago advertising man, a
usually confident guy who was little more than a year
into his marriage, about this notion:

Q: *Ah, did you feel pressured to have sex on your honeymoon?*
A: *Probably. Then again, I didn't, because I didn't have
any problem having sex on our honeymoon. But yeah, I
definitely felt pressure to have sex on our honeymoon—
and on the first night.*

The question that remains in these postmodern, postnuptial times is, Why must there be intense pressure on
newlyweds to have such an awesome, flawlessly romantic time? How did things get to this point, anyway?
One answer is history: there used to be even more
stress. Back in the days when marriage by capture was
the rule and a man swept into the town common (along
with able-bodied groomsmen) to steal his bride, he really did spirit her away. Tradition held that the groom
hid his bride for thirty days to keep her from being re-
taken, while the moon passed through its phases. Meantime, the newlyweds were said to have drunk a potion
made of honey. And so, the "honeymoon." Only back
then there were fears of recapture and death, not of extra bathing suit pounds and mounting credit card debt.

Susie, twenty-seven, a twice-married dietitian from
Reno, Nevada, spoke for many brides when she said
that honeymoons are overrated. "If you're really in
love, you don't need a honeymoon to make things *official,*" she comments. In a way, she's right. But try

telling that to the folks at *BRIDE'S* magazine, hundreds of employees of Hawaiian, Caribbean, and Poconos couples resorts, and hundreds of harried travel agents who every March and October end up booking reservations—for June and January weddings—at a furious pace.

No, you don't actually *need* a honeymoon, but if you skip or postpone yours, you should remember that a honeymoon serves at least three crucial functions in cementing a marriage—or at least its first year:

First, it gives you an escape, allowing you to be together but also away from the stress of *performing* in front of family, friends, colleagues, and "guests" whose dinners you've reluctantly bought when your single friends called four days before the R.S.V.P. deadline, asking if they could bring "this wonderful guy" they just met the week after New Year's Eve. (How could you say no? Usually you don't.) Plus, as Kim, a twenty-seven-year-old publishing assistant who lives and works in New York City, said, "The honeymoon serves as a transitional stage. It gives you time to talk about plans and dreams, and you kind of get used to your new titles of 'husband' and 'wife'!"

Second, if sex is important to you as a couple, a honeymoon can provide a setting in which you may have more sex in one week or two than you may ever again have in that space of time. It enables you to relax with your spouse romantically and physically—and to get reacquainted with each other without the hassles of home.

Third, it gives you a kind of lifelong gauge of your happiness as a couple, set off in a convenient time-and-space frame. As in, "We haven't done this or *that* since . . . our honeymoon, Honey"—which you may one day all too soon hear your husband or wife saying. "I know, Hon," may come the response, "I know." And so it may be, although it needn't necessarily be, a hall-mark of declining expectation.

Getting the Honeymoon on the Right Amtrak

In fact, there are strategies you can use to improve the honeymoon as a vacation, as a relationship-bonding event, and as a truly rewarding time in your lives, irre-spective of the cost or sexual travails you may inevitably recall. Once, that is, you downsize your dreams a little and put them into perspective.

To do that, it helps to consider the saga of Rebecca Roepe and Ben Rosenfeld, two East Coast newlyweds who had spent a year shuttling by train between Philadelphia and New York City in the year of their en-gagement. That and a fear of flying somehow gave them the idea to kick off their honeymoon with a ro-mantic ride by rail from New York, where they were married, to Miami, Florida. Yet if ever there was a hon-eymoon that got off on the wrong track more than Re-becca and Ben's, it probably took place in the movies. For what happened to them one fall day in 1987 all be-gan when Rebecca and Ben hopped aboard an Amtrak train at Pennsylvania Station and settled in. Soon after the ride from honeymoon hell really began.

About five states into their run, and ninety-six or so hours into their marriage, Ben got up to get his wife a drink and snack from the club car. He walked through one car, another, then another, all the while hitting the chest-high automatic door-open buttons with the heel of his right hand, until he smelled pastries warming in the microwave oven on board. He patiently waited his turn in line, which seemed to take a lot longer than it had to, then finally placed his order with the steward (including a cup of tea he was nice enough to fetch for a fellow passenger sitting next to his wife). Once his folding cardboard carrying tray was filled, Ben was off on his return, this time opening the doors between cars using the handy shin-high door switches, which he kicked open with a deft touch of his shoe.

Suddenly he ran out of automatic doors and was startled. He looked around for Rebecca and couldn't find her. He retraced his steps and went the other way on the train but quickly realized when he came to the mail car that he *hadn't* merely gone the wrong way back. Something else was wrong. Something else, indeed.

Rebecca, for her part, was frightened. She remembers thinking the worst—that on the way back for the snacks, her husband of half a day may have stopped between two cars for a breath of fresh air and somehow fallen off the train. (This is the kind of terror that newlyweds, understandably, are prone to have.) But that was not the case, either.

Rebecca, who didn't want to broadcast her fear, got up and quietly asked the next conductor she saw if he had seen a tall brown-haired man wearing glasses and carrying coffee, tea, a Diet Coke and a couple of sandwiches. At about the same time, Ben asked a different conductor to explain the twilight-zone feeling he now had, and it became clear in an instant. While he was waiting for the snacks, the train had stopped at a station in northern Florida, and four cars had been uncoupled and connected to a different engine. Half the train, which Rebecca was on, had headed on to Fort Lauderdale, while the wayward half, which Ben was on, was attached to a new engine and now aimed for Tampa, or some such city.

Ben didn't find this funny. Neither did Rebecca, who laughs about it now. At the time she was almost physically sickened by the chain of events and by the fact that during this, the first week of her honeymoon, which was supposed to be so romantic, she didn't have a clue as to how she was going to meet up with her husband. Or where. And Ben was holding the snacks, fuming to himself and to anyone who would listen, that what was happening to him and his bride could not be possible. It just couldn't. After all, as part of their courtship, right after law school (where they had met), he and Rebecca must have taken the train back and forth between Philadelphia and New York City about a hundred times. Nothing ever went wrong then. Why now?

At the next stop of Ben's train, at the conductor's suggestion, he got off and made some plans. He found out when and where he could catch up with his wife and set about reuniting with her. But by now, traveling by train was out of the question. He would have to rent a car in "Nowheresville," he said, and catch up with her that night, if he was lucky. It was so frustrating it was almost comical. Almost. He had no baggage, no toothbrush, no formal itinerary. And no bride. She was still on the train, waiting for her husband to bring back the beverages and free them from the Honeymoon Hell Hall of Fame. It almost goes without saying that they haven't had an Amtrak vacation since. Almost.

Realistic Expectations?

Danny Jacobson, the co-creator and executive producer of *Mad About You,* the popular NBC sitcom about newlyweds, is the kind of guy who could take Rebecca and Ben's story and put it on screen to be reenacted by his colleagues the actors Paul Reiser and Helen Hunt. But Jacobson himself may not find honeymoon stories of any stripe especially funny. When I interviewed him and asked him about his own, which took place in 1988, he called it one of the shortest on record. On the second night, it was over: "My honeymoon got cut," is how he describes it. Not by sickness or catastrophe—but by Roseanne Barr (who wasn't yet Roseanne Arnold), whom Jacobson worked for as head

"I don't think the honeymoon is over-rated; I think the wedding ceremony and reception are overrated!"

writer in the early days of her eponymous television show. Basically, she got upset about how things were going on the set of the show and got on the phone and *called Jacobson home.* Honeymoon or not, he came home. His wife was not pleased, to put it mildly, but she understood. She is in show business, too.

In a different vein, Tim, forty-four, of Reno, Nevada, married for a little longer than a year, says that his honeymoon was "a great reason for an extended vacation— fun, too! We had a good clue as to who we were as individuals and as a team before we got married, so we got to just play and relax." Playing is something people don't always set aside time for on that all-important getaway, and that's too bad. Real life will catch up much too soon.

"I don't think the honeymoon is overrated; I think the wedding ceremony and reception are overrated!" said Sandie, twenty-nine, a graphic designer and stu-dent, also from Nevada. "Some couples place more em-phasis on these than on marriage itself."

Jean, thirty-two, a social worker from the East Coast who has been married for one year, similarly feels that honeymoons have value beyond simple recovery. Of hers, she said, "It was enjoyable to relax together and to take a vacation together. But as far as a romantic get-away, *that* is overrated in my opinion—by those who benefit financially from selling the honeymoon pack-age. We had a wonderful vacation; we spent time to-gether, and some time with my new brother-in-law, who was with us, along with several wonderful friends of his." (Maybe it would have been more romantic had she not agreed to hook up with her brother-in-law and his wonderful friends quite so soon after the wedding.)

"I found our honeymoon to be more for necessity than a getaway purely for fun," said John, twenty-nine, an insurance adjuster from San Francisco who looked back after having been married just three months. "The preparation for marriage is very stressful, and it was wonderful to get away to relax and reflect on the whole event." John also considered the sexual side of the honeymoon to be quite important because it emphasized, for him and his wife, the "newfound freedom of being together" that they had felt. It's a freedom couples don't always feel so soon after their wedding.

A Bungee Jump into Marriage

Speaking of insurance adjusting and feelings of freedom, Barbara and Geoff, a Chicago couple who chose Australia and New Zealand as two of their honeymoon sites, might have considered speaking with John before they left on their big trip. These two have always tried to pack as much activity as they could into any trip they've taken, and their first overseas trip as a married couple was no exception. When they got to Queenstown, New Zealand, however, they went one further: they decided to go bungee jumping, something neither of them had done before—and this wasn't exactly romantic for the both of them.

As Barbara recalled: "There was this couple we met from Australia, with whom we became fast friends, and while Karen was not going to do it, I, being the brash American, decided, 'Oh sure, I could do that.' And then as we got close to the bridge we were going to jump from, I was, like, 'No way. I'm NOT going to do that.'

Then Karen said, 'Oh, *I* really want to do it now too,' so I was in a quandary: do I wimp out and have her do it and me not do it? No chance." She jumped. "I would say peer pressure and the fact that I really didn't think it was a life-threatening thing to do got me to do it," Barbara said. "It was posed as a very safe, action-adventure outing for us."

Was she scared?

"Oh, I was terrified," she said. "I've never been so afraid in my entire life. Not even in a bad plane ride. I mean, standing on the edge of that platform was the most frightening experience in my life."

Thinking back, Barbara has mixed feelings about her honeymoon antics. She even thinks at times that plunging off a bridge tied to an oversized rubber band was a bit ridiculous. "I mean, I really wanted to do it just to say that I had done it," she said, "or just to have the experience once. But having done it, I am a very fulfilled person now, and I don't ever need to do it again—backwards, forwards, whatever. I would never do it. I would skydive or do something different where there is that adventure thrill. But I would never, never bungee jump again."

When I asked her if she loved her newlywed husband any more after the 240-foot jump than she had before, she said that love really wasn't on her mind at this particular time. "To be honest," she said, "I was incredibly frightened; I was relieved after I did my jump, and I was glad that it was over, but then I had to stand and wait to be picked up from the drop site, and I was on this little island in the river—standing there in the boat that dropped us off there—and just kind of standing, waiting for Geoff to do it, and I thought: 'Wouldn't it be horrible to watch my husband plunge to his death?' And that's all I could think about until he finished—that he's going to jump off here, and I'm going to be standing at the bottom watching him do this and see him, you know, get dumped in the river. It was pretty scary. That was the *second* scariest moment of my life."

Betty, thirty-eight, a Chicago-area mother of two, had a far more sedate honeymoon trip to Italy. Widowed at age thirty-two and then married to her current husband two years later, she spoke with a sense of openness and authority: "I think that people place too much importance on this tradition. It's like any vacation, with highs and lows. For people to look forward to this as the high point in marriage is unrealistic. Some of the best times in my marriage have been when romance has been totally unexpected—on a Sunday night after the ten o'clock news, while it rained outside."

In other words, she added, "I don't need a lei and unending sunshine for backdrops."

"Whooo, married! this is weird."

Katie and Mike, the Tulsa couple (see Chapter 1), didn't necessarily need a lei and sunshine either, but they got them anyway. "Yeah, I finagled a deal," Mike reported. "I had enough [frequent flyer] coupons for two round-trip tickets in coach, and they gave us two first class trips to Hawaii."

"We stayed on Maui; it was great!" Katie said.

"The first couple of days we were both kind of tired," Mike said, "so basically we did what we wanted to do when we wanted to do it. I mean we'd been through so much—"

"Emotionally," Katie interrupted.

"I mean, you're so charged up," added Mike.

"It's neat, though," said Katie. "I mean, you wake up and you're like, 'Oh!' I mean, 'Wow!'"

"It was like, 'This is weird,'" said Mike. "I was thinking, 'Whooo, married! this is *weird.*'"

"And now it's like, I look down and see his ring, and I still do that."

"I do that too," said Mike.

As an outsider (and a newlywed) looking in at their marriage, I found it refreshing—and inspiring—that they finished each other's thoughts and sentences. On more than a few occasions. They even apologized to each other when they did it, but couldn't help it.

"But as for advice, I would say don't plan a lot on the honeymoon," Katie said. "Don't plan a lot of trips and things like that. We didn't have any plans, other than we knew that one day we wanted to go snorkeling. I know that every couple is different and that some people love to travel. But at least for those first couple of days, you know . . ."

"Wait for a while," Mike said.

"Yeah," Katie added. "I mean, we were spontaneous the whole time, and I think it made it a lot more relaxed. We didn't feel like, 'Okay, now we've got to go here and at six fifteen we get on the ship . . .'" Translation: take some time to do nothing during those first few days, because it will inevitably turn into *something*.

Thirty-year-old Helena, of Washington, D.C., who has been married nearly three years, remembers that on her honeymoon, she and her husband, Peter, "needed time to relax, and we got it. I never had an image of wild sex on Hawaiian beaches, so I guess I didn't have high expectations."

Great Sexpectations

Where did all these wild-sex high expectations on honeymoons come from, anyway?

You can't just blame the bridal magazines or modern sexual mores, because if you were to visit the Sex Information and Education Council of the United States library in New York City, you'd find a choice selection of old books about marriage, many of which were published as marriage manuals for couples in the 1940s and 1950s and others from long before. Remember, TV talk shows with all their frank advice and their husbands-who-sleep-with-their-wives'-best-friends topics hadn't been invented yet. These guides were helpful and succinct when it came time to discuss the honeymoon, for they were writing for many a virgin reader at the time. Nowadays, marriage manuals are more about how to fix wounded relationships or how to deal with ex-partners than about how to start up a healthy marriage.

"We think honeymoons nowadays are generally overrated," said Don and Polly of Bethesda, Maryland, who are both in their thirties and who have been married one and a half years. "In this day and age," Polly added, "it means a lot less than it used to because the couple know each other long before this event."

But, of course, not always. One twenty-one-year-old newlywed husband from Reno told me, "I think we had some ideal preconceptions shattered during our honeymoon. Especially ones concerning sex, because we were both virgins going into the marriage."

Honeymoons, then, can still be a time to learn about things, physical things, that you will share forever. After all, in 1 Corinthians 7, Paul wrote:

> *It is well for a man not to touch a woman. But because of the temptation to immorality, each man should have his own wife and each woman her own husband. The husband should give to his wife her conjugal rights, and likewise the wife to her husband. For the wife does not rule her own body, but the husband does; likewise the husband does not rule over his own body, but the wife does. Do not refuse one another except perhaps by agreement for a season.*

In other words, to have *and* to hold.

In a related matter, one problem that millions of couples have faced over the years has been a fear of enjoying sex too much, or perhaps going against the will of the church. How refreshing, then, to stumble upon a holy passage in which marital sex is fairly celebrated, even if in its own restrained manner. And of course, "to touch" means so much more than to touch. Likewise, it's not that Paul was telling couples to refrain from having sex; he was, by many accounts, urging them to become *fully* married—to give their bodies over to their partners in ways they obviously never have before.

In the Jewish religion, teachings of the Talmud similarly instruct the husband to revere his wife and make certain she is satisfied in all respects, including the sexual. Read the fifteen-hundred-year-old writings closely and you may never view religion and sex and honeymoons as rigidly as you did before.

Rachel and William, who are thirty-two and thirty-three and who live in New Jersey, are as upfront about their honeymoon as they are about other parts of their marriage. As Rachel put it, "We lived together for two years, and we had been together for five before we got married. So it wasn't like this was our first opportunity to be together and *go wild*."

William responded, "We went to Italy for a specific purpose: to see more of a country that we both knew we already liked. It just happened to be right after we got married. Big deal."

"I don't think honeymoons serve the same purpose that they used to," Rachel said. "For couples who save sex for their wedding night—okay, fine."

"Beyond sex," William added, "I think in previous generations a honeymoon was the first chance a couple had to travel anywhere *ever* in their lives. Nowadays, if you have any kind of collective curiosity, you probably have traveled together already."

Rosemary and Jim, a couple who live outside of Milwaukee and have been married almost two years, told me that they agreed upon and endured a one-month self-imposed ban on intercourse—and other sex—prior to their wedding and honeymoon. This occurred even though they recently had started living together before the wedding, and not because of their Christian upbringing. While Rosemary considered the idea romantic, especially as the pent-up desire would carry over to the honeymoon, Jim had a slightly different view.

"I think it's bullshit," he told me in retrospect. "And I think that wives who do that to their husbands are bad wives." He sounded as if he was kidding. "She cut me off," he added, "so that it would be special on our wedding night."

And?

"It wasn't that special. I mean it was special because we were married, but it wasn't special in the fact that it wasn't by far the best sex we've ever had."

Which of course made me wonder: was their honeymoon, which was, appropriately, on St. John, in the *Virgin* Islands, extra romantic in their minds?

"Well," Rosemary told me, "a couple of nights in a row, we went out, we swam out at night—like ten thirty at night—and it was a full moon. This was, like, the last three nights we were there; we had either a full moon or an almost full moon all three nights. And we went out, just spent a lot of time just lolling in the shallow water completely naked together. The water was a perfect temperature, and the air was, you know, the same temperature, and that was the highlight of my honeymoon."

In a separate interview, Jim answered the question about romance on their honeymoon by saying, "We went nude swimming on the beach at night. I haven't done that since."

'Nuff said. To the point. Typical male, some might say. But whose idea was it?

"Mine," Jim said. Pause. "Well, the idea to go swimming was both of ours. It was my idea to be nude."

Rosemary and Jim also said, forthrightly, that the best sex of their lives together (at least so far) did not occur on their honeymoon.

"I mean," Jim told me, "I didn't feel tons of pressure on my honeymoon, because we didn't have sex every night."

People often say, I told him, that couples make love more often on their honeymoon than on any other week in their lives. Hadn't he heard all that talk?

"I don't believe that either," he said. "I always thought that the notion of all these married couples who have tons of sex at the beginning and then never have it later on was bullshit and was not something to strive for."

Beyond Honeymoon Cystitis

Tons of sex at the beginning, it should be pointed out, is not always a surefire guarantee of postnuptial bliss. As Vicki Hufnagel, M.D., a gynecologist and gynecological surgeon from Los Angeles, points out, "The first thing that happens in the honeymoon—and into the first year of marriage—and that most men and women don't realize, is that the change in the amount of sex and the way in which they perform the sex creates, for women, high rates of urinary tract infection."

The conventional wisdom in the old days (and even in the not so old days) was that these infections were caused by irritation from friction between the penis and the vagina and from not what people coyly called "overuse." Doctor Hufnagel, on the other hand, often sees fit to challenge conventional wisdom, especially when it involves her patients. "It's all based on poor hygiene and a lack of education, on both the male partner's and female partner's part, on what they need to do to prevent that," she says. In terms of prevention, she tells couples to keep in mind that whenever they have sex and fall asleep for six or eight hours, say, the body's naturally occurring bacteria multiply. "They go up the urethra," Doctor Hufnagel says, "and by then, just because of their sheer numbers, you wake up with a [bout of] cystitis."

In other words, the folklore is misleading: honeymoon cystitis is not about having too much intercourse and all that in the space of just a few days or a week with no break.

"It's not the *too much* sex at all," Hufnagel says, referring to cystitis and urethritis, another common urinary tract infection. "In fact, *not* having intercourse is another way that they develop. Say you get married and your jobs change and you don't see your sweetie for four or five weeks. Then you get together and have a lot of sex. What happens is the vaginal lining has actually changed—it has thinned. In a sense, then, having intercourse every night or every other night can result in more resilient female reproductive organs." (You didn't find this in the marriage manuals of the 1950s.)

To prevent some of these infections, as well as visits to a hotel doctor while on your honeymoon, Hufnagel advises that couples be aware that the vaginal opening is so close to the urethra that germs can travel between them in an instant. Other bacteria also hide out in and around the rectum. So, it happens, a husband's petting and playful stimulation of his bride can put her at some risk for nagging urinary infections. Especially, Hufnagel explains, when a woman has abundant pubic hair.

"Guys are lucky in this regard because they've got a penis, a long urethra, and they don't have pubic hair touching around the opening to the urethra," Hufnagel says. "So they're not at as much risk. That's why it takes so much more for a man to get a bladder infection."

So is there a solution, not just for honeymooners but for other sexually active couples?

"Some women," Hufnagel advises, "I simply tell to shave their lower pubic hair. (They don't have to shave the upper pubic hair.) It can reduce infections enormously."

On other, rarer occasions, women who recently have had a lot of sexual activity, as on their honeymoon, may present their gynecologist with a mysterious complaint: their breasts leaked milk—and they don't have children and aren't even pregnant. It turns out that overstimulation of the breasts, by a partner's touching, rubbing, or sucking of the nipples (repeatedly, for a number of days in a row), can kick off the process of lactation, as if a baby actually *were* suckling. And it is not harmful, doctors say, as much as it can be frightening to the uninitiated. Especially on a honeymoon.

If it weren't so difficult for some doctors to tell their patients this kind of information, Hufnagel says, hundreds of thousands of prescriptions for infections could be avoided. But it's not pretty to discuss, and it is often easier for a doctor to prescribe a series of antibiotics to a patient instead. "It's about being smarter, more educated," Hufnagel says. "I mean, you can probably be *more* sexual. The mystery doesn't make it more sexy at all."

Other Personal Revelations

Aside from the proverbial talk of honeymoons and sex, Rosemary's husband, Jim, said, "I didn't feel that much pressure to have fun every minute while we were together, either. I mean, I did have fun on my honeymoon; it just kind of came naturally, though. If there were times where I was really tired or sunburned or stuff, and I wanted to just lie down and read or something, she was fine with that." (When I asked her later about that, Rosemary—the hyperkinetic partner of the two—agreed that she was able to give in and relax at times.)

"To me," Jim concluded, "the idea of a honeymoon has always been kind of like a fantasy vacation. To do something you've always wanted to do, that you've never done before." You know, like skinny-dipping in the ocean under a full moon.

"Yeah," Rosemary joked. "Honey—moon me!"

On my own honeymoon, on the French side of the Caribbean island of St. Martin, known for its beaches and four star restaurants, there was a lot of topless sunbathing and a little bit of nude swimming. The latter took place mostly on Orient Beach, some three miles from the tiny village of Grand Case, where Paula and I stayed. Being somewhat modest, however, we didn't stroll the beach au naturel. Nor did we go the thong route. *Limited* topless was about as much as we felt comfortable with out in the sunshine.

There were other adjustments we found ourselves making in our first week of marriage, including getting adjusted to "island time." As on Jamaica and assorted other Caribbean isles, you can't hurry love on St. Martin.

When we arrived at Princess Juliana Airport, we were greeted by . . . nobody. Surprise! Our driver from the villa at which we were staying was late. By twenty minutes, it turned out. When he arrived, he introduced himself as Clyde; he smiled apologetically and pointed us toward his Toyota. When we saw that he had a half-opened bottle of beer on his lap as we left the airport, we knew we weren't in New York anymore. Not by a long shot. Strangely, though, we didn't feel in any danger. Call it honeymoon stupor, but we sat back unperturbed and took in the sights, including the herds of goats that roamed the street sides, perilously close to the scattershot traffic that ran along the winding island roads.

If by chance she got pregnant, it would be a good thing.

"The first time it occurred to me and really hit me that things were different between us now was on the honeymoon," Paula told me soon after we returned. "It was like there is a definite line you cross when you get married. You can't just buy something like jewelry at a duty-free shop just because you want it. Now it must become a more responsible decision. As in, 'We've spent so much money on the wedding, and I don't really need it.' Before I was married, if I saw something within reason and I wanted it, I bought it!"

Still another honeymoon revelation for us, maybe more so for Paula, was that if by chance she got pregnant, it would be *a good thing*. All of a sudden it's "legal," and even if we weren't planning a family yet, in the event of an accident it would be okay. It actually put a different feeling on the "I'm late with my period" scare that did in fact arise. And although it turned out to be a case of nerves and stress residue from the previous weeks, Paula and I thought, "You know, if it had been a pregnancy, it would have been all right, even great."

Perhaps not so great, but something that also might

have been expected, was the bout of postwedding blues that struck early on in our honeymoon. Marital therapists, including Susan Rockwell Campbell, Ph.D., of Columbia, Maryland, had warned me in interviews that this is not only common but frequent, yet I was only mildly prepared for it. Fortunately, a forty-one-year-old friend of ours who had been married more than ten years warned us about it too, and it's always easier to accept bad news that comes from a friend.

"We were exhausted and drained from travel and lack of sleep," Paula remembered. "I fell into a blue funk the second day. I didn't know why I felt scared. I had anxiety about what our life was going to be like and whether we would be able to meet the expectations about marriage we had for each other. I even had doubts about whether we did the right thing and if we had discussed marriage enough before we did it."

For my part, I wasn't prepared. And I was supposed to be the expert on marriage, writing a book about it and all. Some expert.

When Paula told me she wondered to herself, "Did we get swept away in the wedding glory and not focus on the *life* of being married?" it was all I could do to remain stoic. Was she implying, without meaning to, that *I* might have been the wrong mate for her? Fortunately, *fortunately,* no.

"I actually felt depressed," Paula confessed. So much focus was on the wedding, and now it was over. What next? Truth be told, I didn't have an answer. She asked me about what our friend had told us about the postwedding blues, and I repeated it: "Don't be surprised if and when they hit." She then thought, "I guess I'm not the first newlywed to lose it!" She also asked me if I felt a bout of that depression, and I said no, because I knew I was ready (at thirty-six) to be married. And I knew Paula was the right person for me.

"Just talking about it together helped a lot," she said. "The freak-outs stopped. We talked a lot about marriage before we did it," she added, "and we will always be great friends, which is so important." Again, the experts on marriage will tell you that. But when you hear it from your wife, on your honeymoon, you believe it.

Chances are, over your many years together, you'll need that friendship. For as Laurie, thirty-three, a grocery clerk from Murphys, California, advised, "The problem with honeymoons isn't about sex." Instead, to her, the problem "is that most couples want to spend more money than they can afford—and so they start out married life in debt."

Which is, as we'll find out in Chapters 7 and 8, another story altogether.

After the Honeymoon

NESTING—AND YOUR NEW HOME

We had to get rid of his sheets—when I thought of all the women who frolicked in them.

—Adelle E., thirty, newlywed bride

*T*hey say that marriage doesn't *really* start until you return from your honeymoon, and they are right—whoever "they" may be. For this is the first time you're actually together as man and wife without the glitter, without the hype, without the distractions of ceremony or vacation, and with all the decisions of starting out still to be made. For most newly married couples, it also means setting up a new home, which is supposed to be fun, which is supposed to be exhilarating, and which often turns out to be exasperating.

You didn't just gain a husband or wife—you gained his or her old sofa bed and chairs, the old posters (from college!), the old T-shirts, the alarm clock that scares the hell out of you when it rings, and boxes of things you may well be fighting about three weeks or months after your wedding day. Including photographs. Especially photographs. And the proverbial bachelor bedsheets.

The point is, you most likely won't be haggling about *things;* you'll be fighting about what those things *mean,* or meant, to you or your spouse. And that will make all the difference.

Suddenly each decision you make becomes a joint decision. Will this fit into your living room or bedroom? Will it fit into your budget? Budget? What budget? You never had one before . . .

Mitch, twenty-six, and Leslie, twenty-seven, of Dallas, felt these changes in their lifestyle a little later in their marriage than Laurie, from Murphys, did. "Basically," Mitch said, "I'd say that three months into your marriage, three months after you're living together and after being together, you find that the responsibilities of paying the rent and paying your bills and keeping out of trouble—just your Average Joe responsibilities—are so different from when you're single. I'm no longer living for myself—I'm living for somebody else, too.

"I have a responsibility to my wife," Mitch added, "to treat her better than I treat myself. I have a responsibility to show her respect and not be late—and to act in a way that will not reflect badly on her later, so people won't say, 'Look at him; who's his wife? It's her!'" Mitch said he felt these new responsibilities grow gradually but firmly as each new week of married life set in. "I have to show her she can rely on me in difficult situations, along with all the little responsibilities," he said.

Another responsibility that newlyweds take on without asking for it concerns their partner's sense of style. For now it is at least *part* of their own. "Before being married I dressed my home and rooms to my taste and style," Laura, thirty-one, from Los Angeles, related. "Now there are two styles and tastes to think about. I remember that looking at art on our honeymoon in the Caribbean was really an eye opener: I love colorful, wacky pictures, and my husband likes scenery types of art. Totally opposite! His colors and styles are more realistic, and much calmer. In a very full store that had shelves and walls full of art, we did not agree on *one* painting that we both liked. Being married, we realized, we're going to have to compromise. A lot. (So we bought no art!)

"Also, even when I was picking up items for my family, things as little as postcards, now I had to think about two families. It's not that it's a burden, or bad. It's just an adjustment."

*W*ith the exception of one couple, none of the wives changed their names.

Another big adjustment Laura had to make was to her new name, since she had decided to add her husband Clark's surname to her own—connected by a hyphen. She had worked for ten years in various jobs, she reasoned, and wanted to keep a semblance of her career identity by keeping her name, even though she wanted very much to start thinking as a couple at home, at work, and everywhere in between. "Most of Clark's friends are married," she said, "and with the exception of one couple, none of the wives changed their names. So at the wedding, several of these women made comments to me and were surprised that I had taken his last name. Maybe it's just L.A.!" Of course, it's not just L.A. where the debate still flickers. And dozens of wives told me they felt it was not fair—or appropriate—for a woman to give up her name, her identity, for a partnership that is supposed to be about unity, sharing, equality.

"To me it was natural and the thing to do to become more of a family," said Laura. "It's not a dishonor to my maiden name, in my opinion. And I think it is an honor to my new bond with my husband. I want to feel that we are united and bonded as one unit. Our children will know they are born into a unity, one solid family. At least that's what I hope for!"

The third big adjustment Laura made in moving in

with Clark as a newlywed wife was, literally, moving. "We had been commuting up and back from L.A. to San Jose [California] for two years before we got married," she said. "We knew we wanted to be together, but someone was going to have to give. His company was based in San Jose, and it would be very hard for him to leave the city and make the kind of money he makes there. Fortunately, I am in a field [video production] that allows me to travel. So it was easier for me to relocate."

At the same time it wasn't easy. Laura said she felt like an interloper trying to find room for her bedroom set, her kitchen pots and pans, her paintings and family photographs, because she moved into an apartment already occupied by her mate. Besides, she missed her friends, her family, even the work associates she used to bitch to Clark about on the phone every night. "You also move into the other person's world of work and friends," she said. "You really feel like an outsider, and it takes a lot of time to feel at home.

"At first I thought, 'I can't live here, I'm giving up my home base, and this just doesn't feel like home,'" Laura said. "Now that five months have gone by, I am starting to feel like San Jose and San Francisco are home, because that is where my new family is. We've spent a lot of time together with his friends, and I feel more a part of their group. I think it's really important just to give it time."

One key point in her adjustment came when Clark realized she was having a tough go of things, about two months after her move. A couple of different times, when they talked late at night in bed, Clark asked Laura, "Do you want to move back to L.A.? We can." Hearing this, she later said, made a big difference in her outlook. "Just knowing that I have that option if I really need to go back," she said, "makes the changes a lot easier to deal with. He really is unselfish and wants me to be happy." She is getting close to happy these days, if she's not already arrived.

"To only expect romance at first is starting out with an element of fantasy that you just can't sustain," said Adelle, thirty, of Nashau, New Hampshire, married three months when we spoke.

Are You Compatible Homebodies?

For fun, or even to stave off future Chair Wars, take this quiz, refashioned from information gathered by BRIDE'S magazine, for the Home Furnishings Council of the United States.

1. In the first year of marriage, I plan to spend the following amount on decorating:

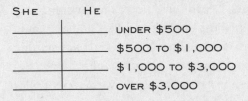

SHE	HE	
		UNDER $500
		$500 TO $1,000
		$1,000 TO $3,000
		OVER $3,000

2. I see myself spending the most time in

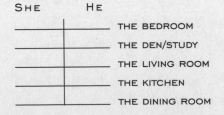

SHE	HE	
		THE BEDROOM
		THE DEN/STUDY
		THE LIVING ROOM
		THE KITCHEN
		THE DINING ROOM

3. Of all the furnishings we acquired by ourselves before marriage, I'd like to keep

SHE HE

_____|_____ EVERYTHING

_____|_____ ONLY MY THINGS; NONE OF MY PARTNER'S

_____|_____ NOTHING, I WANT TO START FRESH

_____|_____ A FEW GOOD PIECES FROM BOTH OF OUR
SETS

4. The mood I envision in our new home is

SHE HE

_____|_____ COZY, COUNTRIFIED, WITH LOTS OF
KNICKKNACKS

_____|_____ CLASSIC, FORMAL, WITH ANTIQUES AND
SILVER

_____|_____ SLEEK, CONTEMPORARY, WITH GEOMETRIC
SHAPES AND CHROME FINISHES

_____|_____ RUGGED, OUTDOORSY, WITH NATURAL
TEXTURES

5. I would like the most visible colors in our home to be

SHE HE

_____|_____ WARM REDS, RUSTS, CORALS

_____|_____ COOL BLUES, GREENS, VIOLETS

_____|_____ GRAPHIC BLACK, WHITE, AND GRAYS

ANSWERS

Although there are no right or wrong answers, there are ways for couples to minimize their conflict when it comes to setting up a home. Some tips from the pros follow.

1. Experts advise you spend no more than one quarter of your annual income on furnishings. Set up a furnishings budget . . . but do so over five years,

not one or two. And force yourself to list the top
three priorities.

2. Break the rules: instead of automatically furnishing the big spaces first, you might get a lot more
enjoyment (use and value) if you decide to fur-
nish a favorite retreat area in your home or apartment first (den, alcove, and so forth).

3. Consider whether some of your older pieces can
be refurbished. Fabrics, repainting, throw pillows,
and the like can buy you extra time and save you
a few hundred needed dollars without sacrificing
much at all.

4. Visit stores, flea markets, and museums to get a
better sense of what you like—your home style, if
you will. You don't have to agree, either: eclectic
is a style, too. You're allowed to mix a few an-
tiques in a modern setting, but don't mix too
many styles. For instance, you might want to stick
with all rustic or all formal styles, even though
they mustn't be matching sets.

5. Think about your favorite colors, both in your
clothes and in the posters or art that you own.
Opposite tastes can work together, fortunately, if
you imagine using cool colors for larger areas, say
(walls, sofas), and more vivid hues for spot color
or accents.

Adapted from *Bride's* magazine; survey conducted for the
Home Furnishings Council of the United States 1991.

Laura's story about resettling on the West Coast
mirrored one I heard on the East Coast, but there
were a few telling differences. For one, when Cheryl,
twenty-four, left her Chicago home to move to her
husband, Michael's, home base of work in Boston,
she had only two years of job experience, while he

had more than five. He was twenty-seven, and had recently gotten a promotion and a transfer, courtesy of his consulting firm, so their decision was more economic than emotional—at first.

Space Invasions

"The first month was the hardest," Cheryl told me. "Michael would go off to work; then he'd walk in the door when he came home, and I was starved for attention. He needed time to wind down, but I was all over him [frequently with complaints]. He felt bad about it; if I missed a friend, he'd say, 'I'm sorry I did this to you.' I said, 'You didn't! *We* did it.' Even so, it took a couple of months until I found a job. In the meantime, I wasn't feeling good about myself. And it upset him to see me lose my self-confidence a bit. He'd say great things, they just didn't sink into me!"

The turning point in their new home was when Cheryl realized that they were *talking* a lot more about things than they did when they were engaged. They discussed their goals as a couple, as a family, each of their career goals—even the proverbial five-year plans they'd always made fun of before. This was so important to Cheryl, she said, "because I'm the kind of person who keeps her emotions in."

What that meant, in terms of her first month in a strange apartment in a strange town in a strange state, was, Cheryl said, "We had all these wedding gifts to deal with, and so I rearranged the cabinets. He couldn't understand why I had to *clean out* the cabinet first, before I rearranged it; he had been living there for a year without me . . . and he never thought he had to clean out the cabinets completely before putting stuff away in them. We have a two-bedroom apartment, but it was set up to be convenient for *him* before I moved in. At first he'd say, 'I can't *find* anything. Where'd you put this—or that?'"

Basically, Cheryl felt as if she were invading his space. But she also told me neither of them used those exact words in the first few weeks of marriage: they would have seemed too harsh, too damaging to what was emerging as an unexpectedly fragile beginning to their marriage. They had never lived together before getting married, unlike a lot of their friends, even though they had gone out for five years. As Catholics, Cheryl and her family didn't approve of couples living together before marriage; the fact that Michael's and her work separated them after college made it that much easier for them to justify living apart—against the tide of their peers, who all seemed to live together for at least a few months of their engagement.

"When we did go out at first, during our first year here," Cheryl said, "a lot of times it was with his friends, and I missed my friends. The thing was, he had been out here first, so he had assimilated—joined a softball team and all that. I was starting over, totally. When I got here, I listened to a radio station one day and started to cry—I *missed* my old radio station in Chicago. I was afraid to come to Boston. I'd seen all the homeless people; it was worse than Chicago. They were even by the Boston Common. Michael would say, 'Why don't you go to museums?' I was afraid, that's why. After our honeymoon, we were going to drive from my parents' home to New England, and *I cried all the way to Ohio!*"

Now, at least, she can laugh when she tells the story. "You wake up the next day and say, '*Wow!* we're married!'" she said. "It's such a *weird* concept. It just blows me away sometimes. But it's a great feeling. I can tell because I feel that even when I'm washing the dishes."

The high point of their first year, Cheryl said, was a

weekend trip they took to Cape Cod, a ferry ride away, which could have seemed boring or trite to weary tourists, but ended up feeling romantic for both of them. "I could see us starting a new life here, finally," Cheryl said. It was perhaps too symbolic, but it was as if they were starting—at three months into their marriage—to build their own history. "I knew then," she said, "that by closing my mind I wouldn't be helping us at all."

Before they got married, Michael made a commitment to Cheryl that suggested to her he was as willing to bend for her wishes as she would for his: he said he would convert to Catholicism, which was not a promise made on a whim to please anybody's parents (his were Lutheran). He went every Sunday to classes for one year; he went to inquiries at the church on Thursday nights; and he told his bride-to-be that he was doing this for her but also for him. If they were going to be married in a Catholic church, he "didn't want to be a bystander."

As for what Cheryl would tell other brides-to-be about that first year at home, "The one thing I would say is to [try to] feel good about yourself. It helps the relationship to grow. If you're strong and you've worked on yourself, you can grow as a couple." The  problem she had to overcome, she found, was that you can't get all of your identity from your partner or you'll start to resent him. As soon as she started feeling confident and self-assured, she and Michael started being able to go out and do their own things, alone and apart from each other. It was tough starting over, she said, "especially because all my other identities (from friends, work, and families) were in Chicago—and we were in Boston.

"The second thing," she said, "is to learn how to

communicate. It sounds clichéd; it sounds sort of strange; but that's how we work on things. He lets it out; I keep things in. Now I'm learning to let it go and get on with it. Once we found out how I did it, it helped a lot. But nobody *told* us about it! All our parents said was: 'It's not going to be as easy as you think. You'll get over it.'"

Around the House: Good and Bad Habits

Uh-oh. The news was not going to go over big with a lot of modern newlyweds: a report from the fifty-first annual meeting of the American Association of Marital and Family Therapists was not exactly good for women. "Guys wed for better, wives for worse," journalist Karen S. Peterson reported in a front-page story in *USA Today*. After talking with six eminent therapists who had gathered in Anaheim, California, to discuss the state of marriage, it turned out five of the six said, basically, that men get a better deal from marriage than women do. Not only psychologically and medically, but also in terms of who does what around the house.

"We have evidence now that even in dual career couples where the wife earns as much or more, she still does the burden of the scuzz work," said Neil Jacobson, Ph.D., a University of Washington psychologist.[1] Big surprise, countless women might say. But it was worth noting that Jacobson used the word "evidence," as if husbands—or the institution of marriage itself—were on trial.

Well, of course, marriage isn't. But the truth is, husbands *are* on trial in the first year of marriage. Wives are too. There's no denying it when you think about it, but people don't think about it all that often: they take the two-lives-merge-into-one part of marriage for granted. They assume things will just, well, *work out*. Fortunately they often do, a lot of the time; but as the majority of couples find out, the merging of lives on a day-to-day, intimate basis is a lot more complex than they thought. From good and bad habits around the home to eating patterns and cooking in the kitchen, to his-and-her bathroom styles and beyond, nesting is testing—each other. It's tricky business, it's tough, but it does have rewards, as you'll see from the disparate true life stories that follow.

"He can't buy vegetables!" Debbie, twenty-six, of New York City, said of her husband, Todd, also twenty-six, during a dinnertime interview. "He doesn't eat them, so he doesn't know how to buy them. I sent him to the store a few weeks ago to get celery, because we were having six people over, and he brought home a tiny package of sliced celery—and carrots—enough to feed two people."

"He'll have Pop-Tarts for breakfast, licorice for lunch . . . and he won't eat salad. I've never seen him eat lettuce," she said. "He's like my *kid* sometimes."

"It tastes like paper," he said, nodding in agreement. "Wet paper."

"He ate snake once, but he won't eat vegetables," Debbie said.

"Vegetables, mustard, and coleslaw," Todd said, as if this were his mantra. Vegetables, mustard, and coleslaw. No, no, never, never. Uh-uh-uh. "I can't be in the same room when Debbie has mustard," he added.

"It is bizarre," Debbie added. "He's like the young one, and I'm like the eighty-year-old in this relationship." She's also been frustrated by this, not surprisingly, because she can't very well cook recipes for two if there's even a hint of greenery or green bean or "wet paper" among the ingredients. She enjoys cooking, so she doesn't see it as a burden or her job, but Debbie can't help but wonder whether this trait of Todd's will be as cute in ten years as it is now. Will she still be in charge of the kitchen?

Jean, thirty-two, a recently married social worker from Reno, Nevada, thought about her own past few months of marriage and said, "Preferably, the couple should divide the household duties at the beginning of the marriage. Otherwise, I've found it [too] easy to assume the stereotypical duties, such as a wife cleaning the house and husband mowing the lawn. When decisions are made about how to divide duties," she added, "it's important for each person to be willing to adjust to another's standard of clean."

Considering Jean's comments, I thought a lot about that last phrase: each other's "standard of clean." She hit right on it. And there is hardly a better example of what it meant than when a Tulsa couple I talked with told me, eight months into their marriage, about a missing key and a living room couch.

"Paul always loses his keys," said Carolyn, thirty-three, a retail store manager, about her husband of ten months, "and when he lost the key to his brother's house a few months after we got married, we tried to retrace all of our steps, because we were house-sitting for him. No luck. So we started [looking] in our house, and when we took all the cushions out of the couch, there was a Snickers candy bar wrapper, and he said, 'There's something in there,' and he reached in and got the candy bar wrapper and said, 'Oh, it was just a Snickers wrapper,' and he *put it back* under the couch cushions. I went, 'What are you doing!?! While we're at it, why don't we throw it *away*?'"

Well, I offered, maybe he was just respecting nature.

"I just went crazy," Carolyn said, "because I am very clean and very organized, and I will have my papers lined up like so, and I swear he'll come over here and move them just a little bit, he'll do it just to aggravate me, because he knows that I'll notice." A little joke, she explained. Very little. "And he saves everything," Carolyn said, "business cards, coupons, just everything, and I always try to go through and throw them away. And he gets furious because he says he was saving them for some reason. But it's not like we have one place where he puts it: it's everywhere. He doesn't see the urgency of doing it, organizing it, and I like to just get it done—let's throw it away as we go, like the Snickers wrapper!"

To be fair, Carolyn conceded that Paul periodically sorts his piles of miscellania and does in fact help clean the house and hang the blinds without too much prodding. It's more his little *habits* around the house that grate on her. "He's not a slob," his wife said. "I mean, he is a clean person."

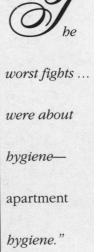

"*The worst fights … were about hygiene—* apartment *hygiene.*"

Stan, thirty-seven, and Dierdre, thirty-one, of Chicago, also had some of the loudest fights of their first year of marriage—most of them, actually—about their differing standards of clean. "The worst fights," Stan remembered, "were about hygiene—*apartment* hygiene, though, not personal. It's like, when I'm home on a day off and she's at work, when she comes home and the place is a mess, she can't understand how that could be." He tries (usually unsuccessfully) to explain that on his days off, he likes to feel as if he's taken them off—fully, in every way, down to the computer games for hours, socks under the coffee table, and Diet Coke cans marking his territory taken during the day.

All of which doesn't jibe with Dierdre, who feels that if he's at home for the day, he should take at least a half hour of that day and get the house in order for her return from a full day of work. Not because he has to, but because it would make her feel good—instead of depressed when she walks in the door, sees the soda cans, and hears the *buh-beep, buh-beep* of the notebook computer games. She also thinks, at times, about the days she has had to ask her husband to shower before he gets into bed after he's been out all day sweating, sometimes on weekends, sometimes after work. "I don't smell myself," he'll say. "That's the point," she'll answer.

How clean is clean?

A couples counselor might analyze this common state of events and say that her anger and frustration isn't intense just because his dirty socks smell. It might go beyond that to the possibility that she may be worried about something else: she may be thinking, without acknowledging it, that she married a man who is (at least part of the time) a slob. Which, by extension, could be considered an expression of *her* judgment, which would then be flawed to some degree. It can get complicated.

In a different vein, Terry Real, a couples counselor and instructor at The Family Institute of Cambridge, Massachusetts, says these kinds of fights and reconciliations serve a purpose early in a marriage. "I like to say that all heterosexual marriages are cross-cultural. So there's a lot of, sort of, duking out over [the likes of] how breakfast gets made—or whether or not you eat breakfast. What are the rituals and the mores? You see, each new marriage is a new family, establishing a whole new set of rules."

"Like when you wash the dishes," I suggested.

"Or *if* you wash the dishes," Real corrected. "Do you wash the dishes right after dinner, or do you let them go until tomorrow morning? How *clean* is clean? Or even stupid things, like whether the window's going to be open or not. Believe it or not, these are intense negotiations."

Real adds, half kiddingly, "I believe that the dual-control electric blanket has probably saved more marriages than couples therapy! And I think this whole business is pretty constant, though subtle, and often has a playful set of notions: 'Is *your* way going to prevail? Is *my* way going to prevail? Or are we going to chuck it and do something that neither of us has ever done before? How's all this gonna work?'"

"Basically, Harry and I are on par when it comes to housework," said Donna, thirty, married eighteen months. "Neither of us is too messy or too clean. We both leave our shoes laying around but at least hang our coats up on a hook."

The only real domestic problem that they have yet to agree upon is the making of the bed. Harry just won't do it and doesn't understand why it needs to be made. "We're just going to sleep in it again and mess it up," he said. Having gone to boarding school as a child and adolescent, his years of regimentation and precise bed making may have left him with a rebellious streak when it comes to comforters and sheets that just won't leave. This frustrates Donna a lot, but he won't budge.

"I'm not even talking about making it fancy," she said. "I'm just talking about pulling the spread up. And I'm not picky," she added. "I remember going out with guys before I got married—one of them had his boots lined up so precisely next to the fireplace that I thought they were a statue. You'd come in and toss your coat on his couch and *fwittt!* it was swept up in an instant and hung up." Without saying so, she implied that such behavior in itself could have been a hang-up to any potential long-range relationship with the stiff, boots-by-the-fireplace guy.

From Clean House to Clean Bodies

Ann and Hal, twenty-nine and thirty-one, are different from Stan and Dierdre. For them, cleanliness and showers are not a problem. They always start their day together in a sensual position in the shower, although sex itself is not a given, depending on their moods. There they are, without clothes, without television or radio noise or other distractions cutting into their shared time together in the morning. They don't always talk much, and that's all right with them both. It's fast becoming a ritual, their ritual, in their fourth month of marriage. And if it sounds romantic, it is. Sometimes.

In a recently published, elegantly designed book, *Massage for Lovers,* author Nitya Lacroix saw fit to include a chapter on showering together, although the editors titled it, rather stuffily, "Aqua Pleasure in Massage." Despite the pretense, the color photographs are pretty to look at, and as Lacroix says, "What then could be more natural than to use the setting of a bath or shower to explore and enjoy our own bodies, or to share the occasion with a partner in an exchange of tender touch?" She goes on to point out that the "luxurious caress" of warm water enables couples to relax in unusual ways, while nakedness and intimacy become more spontaneous and uninhibited than they might otherwise.[2]

She may have forgotten to add that it gets you clean.

In his best-selling book of 1994 and 1995, *Couplehood,* comedian and television sitcom star Paul Reiser says the concept of showering with your partner is, truth be told, all wet. He explains that no matter how romantic the notion might be at the beginning, there comes a time in every twofer shower when one partner is literally getting showered and the other is high and dry over on the other end of the stall. "You got a sweater up there?" Reiser asks. "Maybe a windbreaker? Because," he adds, "no matter how you look at it, at any one time, one of you is not getting water."

On the night Reiser came to the Upper West Side of New York City to sign his witty send-up of marriage, a number of young couples from the neighborhood showed up to get authographed copies. When I saw the wedding rings on one couple's fingers—and when I saw that they were in a long line of Reiser and *Mad About You* fans that snaked through the store like so many college registration lines—I felt compelled to ask about their own patterns of marriage and the realities of living together, from showers to meals to Saturday habits. And they decided to indulge me a little.

"In the shower, when we shower together, he's always freezing," Bonnie, a wife of seven months, said. "There should be two shower heads!" (In fact, in Scandinavian bathrooms, that's not a rare sight.)

"Sometimes I go in there," her husband, Justin, said, "and then I get bummed because I realize, 'What? No play time?'"

When he talks of play time, however, he's not exactly joking. Bonnie told me that sometimes, when they go to bed—promptly at eleven, for her sake—Justin will come to be with her, feign sleep, and then get up and out of bed and pad into the living room to play Sega Genesis on the television. Because he's not tired yet and he doesn't want to annoy his wife by *not* going to bed with her in favor of a video game.

"He always tells me the next day that he played Sega," Bonnie said. Meanwhile, in the mornings, when Justin has the chance to sleep in a bit longer and Bonnie is getting ready for work, she wakes him up every day at six thirty and makes him get out of bed and go into the living room to sleep his last hour and fifteen minutes on the couch. Why? "Because the only good mirror in the apartment," Bonnie said, "is on the back of the bedroom door," and she can't put on her makeup if he is going to traipse to and from the shower, to and from his closet. Taking it in stride, Justin obliges her. Or at least he has in the first few months of marriage. These are the kinds of quirks that newlyweds put up with because they're newlyweds, and they don't really need better reasons than those to help influence their behavior.

In terms of other, perhaps stronger stresses associated with newlywed life, Ellen McGrath, Ph.D., an expert on depression who represents the American Psychological Association from time to time, says that millions of women today aren't working just one or two jobs but three: a day job; household and family chores when they get home; and the "enormous burden" of relationship maintenance that takes place (to some degree) at all times.

One Colorado Springs couple, John and Daryn, who struggled through this phase—and perhaps are still struggling through it—told me they were surprised at how intense some of their feelings were about what they had thought would be "just plain stuff" at first. Turned out it was more than that . . .

"When we moved, it was into John's house, and we used everything of John's," Daryn said. (Everything of Daryn's is either in storage or still at her condo, which is being rented.) "He wouldn't even let me bring my cat. It's very one-sided, but we are looking for a new house.

"And," she added, "we are going to buy a new bed, so we have a bed together, rather than John and Pam's bed."

And who is Pam? I wondered.

"His ex-fiancée," Daryn said, anger rising. After all,

she moved into a new home, right after getting married, and there's an ex-fiancée's bed in the place—or at
least a bed that was bought by both John and this
woman of his past. He claimed that he and Daryn
would soon get rid of it, but not right away, since it
was brand-new and they had debts from the wedding
to settle anyway.

"Get rid of it," therapist Terry Real told me, in a later
interview, when I presented him with this scenario.
"Take an axe to it!"

For her part, Daryn noted that at least the couches
weren't remnants from John's aborted engagement—he
bought those all by himself, after Pam had moved out.
Still, annoying for Daryn, some of Pam's decorating
touches remain. "I mean," Daryn said, "we have all our
wedding stuff out, but that's about it. I had brought a
few plants and stuff, and I've kind of put a woman's
touch to it. But I haven't done anything drastic. That's
why we are looking for a new house—so that it will be
our house." (She later explained, out of earshot of John,
that when he refers to "*this* house, it's *his* house. But
when we refer to the condo, it's *our* condo." Fortunately, she could laugh at this, and did.)

"It was real hard merging," Daryn added, "because,
well, what toaster do you give up? What mixer do you
give up, you know? But a lot of John's stuff never got
used; his washer and dryer was never used prior to me
moving in." He lived like a bachelor after his fiancée
moved out, Daryn said, so he needed to resettle into
his own house, too. Even though he's owned it for
three years, she said.

To be sure, there were psychological adjustments to
this "stuff" beyond what was whose. "*Everything* was
new, you know," Daryn said. "I had to learn that it was
ours, no more his-and-mine, hers, theirs, whatever. It's
ours."

When it came to jobs, though, things were a little different. Daryn left her office manager's job in a retail firm where she had worked for eight years to help John run his contracting firm out of their home office. "It was fine, because I wanted to do it," she said. "I felt that me helping him with his business was really important—because the stress of running it himself was getting to him. It was becoming so overwhelming [it was changing him]—so I felt a need to help him not be so overwhelmed."

While she was still working full-time at her job, Daryn would come home from work and John would ask her to help him with his for three or four hours. Plus there was dinner to cook, which somehow fell to her, even though they both were working. "And clean house, and do laundry, and it just wasn't working," Daryn said. "So it was more feasible for us for me to stay home and work."

A number of other wives I spoke with expressed surprise at the fact that they were expected to do double shifts at work and at home—not because they were blind to tradition but because of a new twist on the so-called traditional values: they told me it made sense, as in Daryn and John's case, that if one spouse was the primary breadwinner, the other spouse should at least consider taking on more of the responsibilities around the house, from cooking and cleaning to bill paying. But more than a few of the wives said they were frustrated by the fact that even when they were making the same amount of money as—or more than—their husbands, they were still expected to carry more than their share of domestic duty. Which was not in any of the postfeminist house rules of order the last time they checked.

On the other hand, a few of them said, if they didn't take the extra chores on, they wouldn't get done. Simi-

larly, if they didn't play the good corporate wife, it
wouldn't be worth the discomfort or resentment they
would likely face so early in their marriage. You pick
your roles—and your battles. For instance, "We have a
second bedroom," Daryn said, "and it's like the junk
room—it's the room from hell. You cannot get *into* the
second bedroom. . . .

"Well, I went in there the other day and I cleaned it
all out. Now you can sit on the bed. There's a full bed
in there, I mean a full bedroom, a beautiful bedroom.
But it had been sitting there cluttered for two years.
Now I've gotten it all cleaned out and organized,
and we can utilize that space instead of just closing the door when people come over. Some of it
was wedding junk," Daryn said, and some of it
was boxes pulled out that just needed to be
shoved back in—"and old clothes he hasn't worn
since like the Sixties at least!"

When I asked her if could give some advice to
other young married couples who feel as if they
too are going through a thousand changes at once
on the home front, Daryn said she thought it had
helped to not automatically slip into the standard
mine-versus-yours territory debate. She obviously
had deep-seated feelings about it, as you can tell
from her comments above, but she thought it
wouldn't have helped them this early into their marriage
to get into fights about "just stuff."

Many couples counselors would disagree with Daryn's
thinking, because they believe up-front is usually the
way to go, especially when the negotiations are about
"stuff." There's less at risk in those situations, and it
gives the partners a chance to develop their own sense
of self within the partnership. Not to mention their
fighting styles.

"I think it pays to be patient," Daryn said, "and kind

Married couples ...feel as if they too are going through a thousand changes at once.

of let things happen the way they happen. Don't be so quick to jump in and say, 'This is mine, and we have to do something with it,' you know? It's hard to explain, but if you try to be understanding, it will work out."

Daryn knew something that day, apparently. For when I talked with her and John four months later, John was giddy on the phone: "We had a garage sale," he said. "You'll never guess how much we got for our stuff."

I was just about to say $250 when he cut me off: "Over a thousand dollars!"

More important, he went on to say, "I sold my bedroom set. For five hundred dollars."

The interesting thing was not that he sold his bedroom set for $500 but that it happened to be *the one* that was picked out over two years ago by Pam, his ex-fiancée. Which means his wife, Daryn, finally won this battle of the possessions—she who could not fathom sleeping on a bed that was chosen by another woman, especially another woman who had slept with and nearly married her now husband, the soon-to-be-father of their child, which was due five months from the time we spoke. So they were then, as it's said, planning for parenthood. A Christmas baby, if all went as expected, would mean, of course, more changes, more stuff, and new furniture in that old second bedroom. These adjustments at home do mean a lot more than opening wedding presents, sending the thank-you notes, and finding a place for the third or fourth pair of candlesticks. And you can't always plan ahead as to which ones will be easy, which ones a little or a lot more difficult.

Evenings at Home...and Solutions, Forever

"When I get home," Adrienne, thirty, of Cambridge, Massachusetts, said, in speaking about some of her first-year adjustments, "I like to get undressed alone. I like to get rid of the turbulence of the day. I try to be like a regular person, instead of the tough bitch I have to be sometimes at work, who's trying to change everything at the office from the slow-paced way it used to be. That's what I was hired to do, and so when I come home, I need a chance to drop my shoulders."

"When I get home," her husband Ed, thirty-two, countered, "I am ravenous, starving. And through the first month of our marriage, when I got home earlier than she did, I *thought* I was doing her the biggest favor—by cooking for her and holding a bowl of food out that was all ready when she walked in the door. She kept rejecting it out of hand." Although Ed didn't say it exactly, he saw this as a slap at him, not just a rejection of the pasta with pesto sauce.

"He was home earlier than I was, a lot," Adrienne said. "And it was summer. When I got home I was dripping with sweat. I couldn't *handle* dinner right away. Plus I was talking to people all day; he wasn't. I was looking to decompress, partly because I lived alone for many years. I apologized for being grouchy, but I was grouchy."

"It took a while for it to sink in," Ed said. "That she was rejecting my food and not me. It's crushing to be rebuffed like that. I felt awful." He felt he was keeping up his half of the partnership, and she was afraid to say something hurtful to him aloud. Trouble was, he still felt awful.

Moving from the kitchen to the bathroom, another site of key newlywed adjustment at night . . . Suzanne, thirty-six, of Columbia, Missouri, said she and her newlywed husband, Mark, forty-two, didn't have the traditional toilet-seat jousting after they moved in together. No, having both been married once before, they moved right on to something more spiritual, something deeper: the battle of the toothpaste tube. "He likes it to be clean and neat, rolled up from the bottom," Suzanne said. "And I could give a shit. I always squeeze it from the middle, and it drives him wild. He makes a point of showing me how to do it (as if I don't know) and how to squeeze it to keep it clean at the top, but I *like* having it messy and crusty near the cap. It's more like life. Life isn't clean!"

They negotiated a truce in their toothpaste tube war with a brilliant solution, one that goes highly recommended and costs less than $22 extra a year: they have, along with their robes and towels, his-and-her tubes of Tartar Control Crest, one neat, one messy, side by side on the bathroom counter. Other couples splurge and buy the neater and more expensive pump tubes.

Oftentimes these mini-fights over silly things take place *instead* of more serious conflicts that may need to come to the surface later on. The toilet seat and toothpaste wars occur so often because partners— whether they realize it or not—need to test how much control they can have over the other person. And control is also a subconscious issue: once it attains a balance between partners, the rest of the squabbles can and often do become just that, squabbles. They become less troublesome and less significant.

"I take it to a much more abstract level. Because it's really not about *things* or about how Christmas is spent," therapist Real says. "It's about turning two 'I's' into a 'we' and the painful process of doing that. And part of that's very concrete: if you have a bedroom set from your old girlfriend, [your wife is going to ask,] 'Am I going to sleep in that bed?' The answer is, 'No I'm not.'

"But it's also about 'I'm religious and you're not,'" Real says. "Or one partner who says, 'I believe that a healthy couple has a lot of contact with family of origin and you can't stand your parents.' Or, 'I have kids from a previous marriage.' So it's really about more than just blending your things. It's also about blending your mores and your cultures and your values, and how each of you gets things done."

The real question, then, is, How will you, as a newly wedded couple, handle the inequity of jobs, chores, and kitchen responsibilities that are destined to occur? There is no such thing as a truly fifty–fifty marriage. Neither marriage nor life works that way. Do you know anyone who does exactly half the cooking, half the cleaning, half the bill paying, and the like? It's not only impractical but theoretically impossible.

Which is another way of saying this is the time to stake out your turf, to make some mistakes as a couple running a home together—it's allowed.

As Terry Real says, "I do a lot of couples work where I give a lot of support to the slob—because the clean one is the one who always gets societal approval. So I tell the slob to stand up for his or her creativity." To even things up at home once in a while.

In other words, *Vive la différence.* But it would still be a good idea to pick up your socks.

The
Secret Spouse

THINGS HE OR SHE NEVER TOLD YOU . . .

AND WHY

You never should have married me. You have all these secrets!

—Harper Pitt to Joe Pitt, in *Angels in America,*
Tony Kushner's award-winning Broadway play

verybody has secrets. That is no secret. But after a newly married couple settles into their first home, sometimes within weeks, sometimes after a few months, certain secrets unfailingly emerge that one partner didn't *quite* get around to telling the other. Or maybe they were things he or she never intended to tell the other. Either way, once the secret is out, the dance begins. Footing becomes shaky, at least for a time. Then a negotiation ensues, or a fight breaks out. It all depends on what the secret was— and why it didn't emerge earlier in the months of dating and engagement. However big or small, the secret issues—now that they aren't secrets any longer—need to be resolved. What follows is how a half dozen couples exposed their secrets and then resolved the matter: from supposedly innocent hidden photographs of exes to sexual longings that perhaps never should have been expressed. (You can be the judge.)

But before we examine these secrets, a preview of sorts is in order. As Jay Hurley, a wardrobe consultant for *Home Alone, Nine Months,* and other films, tells the story, a female friend of his who had recently gotten married had a problem. An inveterate shopper, she felt guilty now about buying more clothes than she needed. Whereas her husband had no problem with her spending a few hundred dollars every few months on jackets, outfits, and shoes, she was used to charging up to a thousand dollars or so in that same span. It was a guilty pleasure, she told Jay, but she also knew it was one she did not want to own up to or give up. She was afraid her husband might not see things her way, as evidenced by the fact that, since their wedding, he had put them on a strict budget to help pay off the wedding debts.

Her solution?

On the way home from Macy's, Nordstrom, or Lord & Taylor, she would secretly drop off the dresses or suits at the cleaners and voilà! The next time she saw them, they were cleaned, pressed, free of shopping tags, and, most important, covered in the familiar plastic sheathing that would raise no spousal suspicion whatsoever. Sly? Yes. Clever? Yes. Sneaky? Yes. Unseemly? Well, maybe. But this is the kind of secret that won't likely harm a marriage; it will at worst test it—if and when the separate credit card bills get mingled or if a husband gets to be as observant about clothes as Jay Hurley happens to be.

One Picture Worth a Thousand Quarrels

In another marriage, in another town, in another couple's closet, a different secret recently became known during a fairly stressful time—moving day. As it happened, Abby, thirty, and Hal, thirty-two, were finally getting around to packing up "Hal's" apartment in Washington, D.C., where they had lived for the first few months of their marriage and where he had lived for four years prior to their engagement. Toward the end of a sweltering August afternoon ("Aren't all August afternoons sweltering—when you're moving?" Abby said), Abby found out that marriage was at least a little more than she bargained for.

"Now I realized that the guy I married has a secret stash! A series of photos of former girlfriends."

"It was ninety-five degrees," she said. "The movers were in the apartment—waiting for us to finish packing—and we were starting to worry about when the *other* people's movers were going to come. Then, in the back of his closet, I came across this half-hidden shelf and a blue pouch that had some photographs in it—"

"I put it there in the darkest corner on purpose," Hal interrupted. "It wasn't like a shrine! It even had a paint scraper in it."

"That's true," Abby said. "For a minute, because of the paint scraper, I thought it was the landlord's stuff just sitting there. But I decided to steal a look at the photographs in the pouch, and when I looked closely at one, I saw it was Hal with a doe-eyed girl. There was another one where he had his arm around a girl I didn't recognize.

"Now I realized that the guy I married has a secret stash! A series of photos of former girlfriends." At this point of the story Abby paused, not only for story-telling effect, but also, I suspected, to remind her husband of the pain he inadvertently had put her through that day.

"Part of me didn't have the heart to throw them out," Hal said, breaking the silence. "So Abby said, 'Why don't you keep them at your mother's?'" At this point in our interview, Hal felt compelled, for his part, to bring up an old photo that Abby has kept in her photo collection that shows her "with an Australian guy . . . she's

smiling broadly . . . plus, he's carrying her. I always wonder, 'Did she have a better time with him? Is that why
she's keeping this around?'" (Abby's trip to Australia was
five years before.)

In truth, both partners were keeping old photographs
around because they were and are meaningful. There is
nothing wrong with keeping such mementos as possessions—it's just that they shouldn't be prominently dis-
played. At the same time, they shouldn't be *too* well
hidden, which will no doubt arouse suspicion if and
when they are stumbled upon.

"What bothered me," Abby said, "was that I felt, if he
needs to keep these things secret, then he's holding
back." She paused. "And that he probably likes her better!" Well, no, he doesn't. And that's why the photo al-
bums are now in a cardboard box in Mom's basement.
Safe and secure and out of the way. For now. . . .

A Soft-Porn Secret

At first it simply sounded unbelievable. Especially
because it was me saying the words that were so hard
to believe. "I knew you'd find it," I said. I wasn't kidding. We hadn't been married two months when my
wife Paula found an issue of *Playboy* magazine I had,
literally, kept under wraps. Yes it was mine, and yes, I
had kept it tucked under a pile of folded T-shirts on the
third shelf of my armoire, even though we had a per-
fectly good oak magazine rack in the living room. But I
didn't hide it so she'd *never* find it; I just hadn't thrown
it away yet and didn't know whether I would be allowed to have *Playboy* in our house—since we had
never talked about such things and had only lived together for a few months before we got married.

I kept it a secret because I wasn't a proud reader of

the magazine. But I also was not ashamed to say that I bought it three or four times a year. For the *cartoons*. Joking aside, though, what Paula most objected to was the secretive nature of my stash. Why hadn't I, she asked, simply stuffed the magazine in with all the *Esquire, GQ, SELF,* and *Outside* magazines that filled the magazine rack in our living room? She had a good point. What was I hiding, really? Guilt? Or guilty pleasure?

I tried to explain—and this was true—that I had never bought a copy of *Playboy* until my thirties (although a number of my roommates had over the years). And when I did so, I wasn't buying them to replace the role of women, my wife in particular, in my sex life. For me the magazine is a guilty pleasure. Other people like Ben & Jerry's chocolate chip cookie dough ice cream. To Paula, though, the photos of nudes were degrading to women and present them as objects, not real people. She questioned my need for looking at them. She felt that I might expect her to look like those photos, even though I assured her repeatedly this was not the case.

I enjoy looking at the photos for the variety, I said. They are appealing and fun diversions, and they do spark some sexual feelings, I added, even though I would never expect my wife to pose like them or look like them. They are models. My wife is real. It's like the movies, I reasoned, appealing to her sense of professionalism (she works in the movies). She knows all too well that sometimes movies include nude scenes for reasons of marketing and allure when the plot doesn't demand them. I also pointed out that my female boss at the magazine I help edit wrote the mega-seller *How to Make Love to a Man* and that she has mentioned *Playboy* in idea meetings on occasion. In addition, each of the three books I've written contains at least one chapter about sex and sexual behavior (see Chapter 6). However I felt about the content of *Playboy,* I reasoned, the fact is, it hits a mainstream chord of male sexuality that I should be familiar with. Finally, I pointed out that I am among a minority of Americans who can deduct the cost of these magazines from my taxes as research expenses. So I may have been buying them for reasonable reasons. But Paula wasn't buying my explanations. She still doesn't. And it's not all about feminism, either.

Our discussions continued for months and ended with one compromise: no more *secret* stashes. I could buy them but could only keep them for one week; then out the door they go, into the recycling pile. "And keep them out in the open if you're not ashamed of them," Paula said. "Okay," I said, "I'll get rid of them after a few days," realizing that in answering her I didn't *quite* agree to keep them out in the open. That's going to take a little more reasoning. And maybe a little more time. There may be no more secrets here, but apparently there's still a glint of hidden shame.

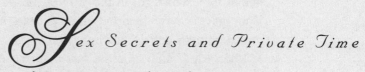

Sex Secrets and Private Time

Marty Klein, Ph.D., is an unusual sex therapist and author from northern California. He is unusual because he not only counsels couples; he also counsels *other* sex therapists at national meetings of sex educators. Which would make him, arguably, the guru to the sex gurus. In any event, Klein believes that when you share some of your sexual experiences with loved ones or good friends, the sharing in and of itself can enrich each partner individually as well as the relationship. At the same time, Klein says, keeping a few secrets from time to time can allow partners to develop a sense of pride and dignity about their past that can go so far as to have healing qualities.

In a recent magazine article, Klein summarized some of the findings he collected in his frank and, frankly, helpful book *Sexual Secrets: When to Keep Them, How to Share Them.* He proclaims: "Common sexual secrets involve: specific sexual preferences, the fact that we masturbate, the true level of our sexual desire, performance fears, fantasies, faked orgasms, sexual dissatisfaction, features of our bodies we're embarrassed about, current or former affairs, a previous pregnancy, abortion or sterilization, a sexually transmitted disease, a past we're ashamed of, or old traumas, such as rape and child abuse."[1] What's startling here is the sheer variety of possibilities: after all, these are just the secrets Klein calls "common"!

As so many of these experiences have negative connotations that don't fade with time, it's not surprising that secrets take on bad feelings—which only encourages a partner to keep them buried, hidden, safe, where they won't get in the way of the here and now. That may not be healthy thinking, but it's far more prevalent than you'd imagine.

When Klein mentions the fact that masturbation is a common sexual secret between partners, he doesn't touch on what happens when that specific secret is exposed. When one couple I talked with stumbled upon the subject, the husband said, "I have no problem talking about it," but his wife hushed him and tried to change the subject. In the case of another young couple, it was disastrous. According to psychiatrist and sex therapist Avodah Offit, M.D., of New York City, "I had a patient who woke up one night to find her husband masturbating in bed next to her and found it such a terrible shock that she went into a state of panic. She had enormous feelings of betrayal: I actually had to make a house call to calm the situation down."[2]

Offit also speaks of another patient she had who was obsessed with the details of her husband's masturbation: where he did it, how often, what time of day. This woman needed to know these details before she could reconcile herself to his furtive habit. He, however, didn't necessarily see it as secret sex or a substitute for her company. Instead, he saw it as private pleasure.

Must We Tell Everything?

Secret pleasures or not, the question still haunts: *everything?* Must we tell each other everything? For Vincent, thirty-four, and his wife, Lucy, twenty-nine, of San Mateo, California, the answer for now is no. At lcast as far as Vince is concerned. In short, he has not told his wife—and cannot tell his wife—that back when he was single and living in Los Angeles, and long before the Heidi Fleiss era, he went to a prostitute. All right, three times. There, he said it. But it was a lot easier to tell me than his wife, he said. She knows all about his old girlfriends, his bathroom habits, his darkest fears about his health, fears about his job in a shaky computer-related business, his embarrassment about having a smallish penis. This stuff all had come out in their engagement or in their first year of being married.

But when he talked with me about the prostitutes—he went to them when he was in his mid-twenties and was quick to tell me he wore a rubber (twice he did; the other time there was no intercourse, "just a hand job")—there was a hint of resignation and guilt in his voice. It seemed he was thinking: since he hasn't told her yet, he doesn't think he ever will. And he would like to, if only to get rid of the guilt.

Except that, "There's no way," he said. "She comes from this great big family, we had a strict Protestant wedding, and I just don't think she needs to know. She might even suspect, for all I know. But if she knew about it, it's not that she would leave me or anything. She would just think I'm a piece of shit. She's never asked. And I'd probably lie if she did."

As far as details go, they're not all that shocking or important, according to Vincent: he was between girlfriends at the time, not dating at all, and he was drunk. He was horny and bored, he added, and he thought these few times would make him feel better about himself. Which they didn't. The settings were seedy (two hotels and a car), the prostitutes weren't what you'd call sensitive, and each time he did it he felt as if he were in a bad movie. So it's no surprise the sex that took place was bad. What is surprising to Vincent is that things that happened during a dark period of his life should still be hanging around ten years later, during such a *light* period, during a time when he and Lucy are buying a house and really settling in as a couple.

"Maybe it's because it's the only *real* secret," he says. Perhaps predictably, when in a separate interview I asked Lucy about her past and her secrets, nothing nearly so dark emerged.

Terry Real, Ph.D., of the Family Institute of Cambridge, Massachusetts, has heard this kind of confession before: when one spouse has something to hide. So he doesn't give a snap answer to the question of whether or when Vince should confess this or other secrets. "You see, [one] notion I have," Real says, "is that I don't believe that honesty in a relationship—and this has to be stated carefully—I think that honesty has to be handled in a sophisticated way. I'm not advocating lies, but if you're really bugged by the fact that your wife is about five inches shorter than the kind of women you're normally attracted to . . . then I don't know that it's in the service of the relationship, necessarily, to share that with her. That may be something that you [should] process inside yourself. Or, you could tell a friend.

"This idea that everybody is supposed to tell everybody everything," he adds, "is one of those ideal notions that actually gets people into some trouble sometimes."

Real is not as cynical as he may sound. He believes, in fact, that many couples handle their relationships with a level of sophistication and nuance that is more complex than our images of where we think we're supposed to be in marriage. "So," he says, "there's a place for privacy in a relationship. There's a place for discretion in a relationship—as in, 'I really want to tell you that the first two years I dated you I was more sexually attracted to your sister than you . . .' I mean, do I really need to say that? Is that really going to further our intimacy?" He doesn't think so.

A Secret Old Romance, Sort Of

Jennifer and Tim, twenty-four and twenty-two years old, are recent newlyweds and college graduates who live and work in Phoenix and who are, not surprisingly, still working on the finer points of intimacy. They lived together for eight months (five of them during their engagement) before they got married one recent afternoon in May.

"The first thing we found out about each other that we hadn't known is that we have differences—real differences—in sleeping," Tim said. "She needs ten hours of sleep every night. If she doesn't get it . . . she's dead; she's got the big ole bags under the eyes, the whole thing."

"I found out we're both really kind of obsessed with the computer," Jennifer responded. "I don't know if I knew that about Tim before."

It turns out Tim and Jennifer had bigger secrets, but they didn't emerge at first. It was easier to talk about sleeping habits and computer obsessions, especially when the real secrets in their marriage pack a lot more emotional wallop. For instance, Tim didn't find out until after they were married that on the night of their very first meeting at a party, he was merely a backup boy Jennifer had invited in case her date that evening turned out to be a loser. "She actually had invited somebody else to come to the party," Tim said, "and then she met me later and dumped him after that."

"He thought he was my main focus," Jennifer said of Tim, smiling, "but it's not that he was the fall guy. I wanted this other guy to come over and he couldn't. And I didn't know Tim, really. I just saw him on campus and thought he was cute, and I wanted to get to know him. So I asked him to come to the party." When her number one date didn't show, Jennifer swung into action toward Tim—not for romantic reasons, she said, but simply so she could "know who he is." Thus she surmised, "It's not really by default."

Did Tim feel at all flattered when he eventually found this out—years after the fact?

No way. He said he felt "kind of shafted. Kind of 'gapped.' Like I was the 'Go-To Guy.'"

Before I could ask Tim to elaborate on any other secrets he might have learned about his wife, Jennifer went on the offensive. Maybe this was because she felt guilty having kept a piece of her personal past from her eventual husband. In any event, she accused Tim of keeping a shadier secret from her. As in: she recently discovered that a female friend of his was not always merely a *friend*.

"I learned about people he was friends with now that I *thought* he was always just friends with but whom he actually had dated," she said. "And he never told me." Putting it bluntly, Jennifer said that finding this out "made me feel kind of weird. Because I graduated before him, and this other girl was still at school with him. She was coming over all the time and was always at the same parties we were at. I never thought anything of it. Then after all this happened, he told me, 'Well, yeah, I dated her.' And I was, like, *'What?!'*"

Trying to get at the root of this common problem among newlyweds, I wondered why Tim didn't see fit to come clean about his old girlfriend, maybe even in a joking manner. It turns out, Tim said, he and Jennifer have completely different views of how open they needed to be about ex–boyfriends and girlfriends. Especially because "I'm friends with all my ex-girlfriends and Jennifer isn't," Tim said. "And so I didn't feel that it was an issue. I mean, I went out with a girl in high school for two months or whatever, and it didn't work out, and we're still friends. And she ended up going to the same college I did, and we're still friends. It was just no big deal."

To him, that is.

As Jennifer explained it, the old-friend secret blew up into a bigger confrontation in part because nothing like this had ever unfolded between them. She was caught unaware and unprepared. When she asked Tim, "Why didn't you ever tell me?" and he said it was no big deal, she wondered what *might* have happened if, say, he had invited this woman to stay overnight on a weekend trip she was making through town. Fortunately, this didn't happen. "It just never came up," she said. "And he's right, you know. I never said, blatantly, 'Did you ever go out with her?' So he never actually lied to me.

"If it was something like that, if he actually had lied to me and said no, and then I found out later—*that* would be important."

In a recent story in *SELF* magazine entitled "Secrets of Intimacy," psychiatrist and author William Betcher, M.D., introduced a few important concepts about privacy that ordinarily go undiscussed. For many couples, the ideas he raised might prove to be helpful in private discussions well beyond the first year of marriage. For instance, Betcher points out that while privacy is considered to be one of our basic rights (it's even part of our Constitution), we often give it up. When you get married, intruding on a spouse's privacy—for better or worse—becomes a right of the *other* spouse. "We feel betrayed if we are not told our partner's innermost secrets," Betcher says. When I asked Doctor Betcher about the secret fantasies that millions of individuals hold inside, both as single and married persons, he said that couples don't necessarily have to share these desires to achieve intimacy.

Probably most important these days are sexual secrets, because of the potential health risks associated with sexually transmitted diseases, and also because of the degree of import sex has taken on in so many modern marriages. As Tim suggested, "Sexual things should be set down long before you get married to each other. With the onset of AIDS and things like that, you have to know a certain amount about [your mate's] sexual history . . . a lot about it. I mean, Jennifer was allowed to be a person in the past; I don't want to hear all the gory details. But I do want to feel safe in being able to be with her."

So on the one hand, you, like Tim, have real concerns about safety and security—a need to pierce your partner's secret shell. You want to be able to let your guard down totally in order to be sexually free. In short, you don't want any sexual secrets anymore. None. On the other hand, you want to allow your partner to have and to cultivate some sense of self, a secret self, if you will, because it seems healthy, wise, and the right thing to do. So then, are you stuck? Must one decision be wrong and the other be right? Not necessarily. There is a way to achieve the right balance between privacy and intimacy, closeness and distance. You can negotiate it, unfamiliar as it may seem.

"People often confuse privacy with secrets," Betcher says. "A secret is covert in a way that privacy is not—it is a decision to withhold your partner's consent or knowledge. By contrast, when a couple agrees for something to remain private, each member has given a *gift* [emphasis added] and gained a measure of freedom. . . . We keep something secret to avoid emotional pain."[3]

Was it a Lie, A Secret, or Both?

For Tom, twenty-six, and Barbara, twenty-five, of Philadelphia, who dated briefly back in high school and then went off to different colleges, the past was never as important as the here and now. Their fling in high school was not what you'd consider unusual for high school romance: a few months, a dozen or so dates, sex but no intercourse, and then other interests intruded before teenage "like" could turn into anything like long-term love and commitment. Besides, Barbara had other commitments in mind: she was determined to do well in college, and the fact that she picked the University of

Pennsylvania meant that she was setting herself up to face Ivy League pressure and competition when it came to classwork. Tom, on the other hand, chose Rutgers University, in New Jersey, a fine state university but not Penn's equal.

"Education is important to me," Barbara said. "Not which school so much as what it does for you. When I thought about getting serious with someone, I wondered, 'Could this person *talk* with me about things?'" It was clear she was thinking of someone who had some worldly interests, although she stopped short of saying her future partner had to have gone to college. Tom, of course, went.

The only trouble was, he led Barbara to believe he had graduated from Rutgers the same year all of his friends did, when in reality, "I went for four years—I was just twenty-five credits short." The way he had it figured, he didn't *need* to graduate, because he was going into his family's contracting business, and that didn't require a degree. Then, after ten years or so—or maybe sooner—he planned to tell his wife about this omission in his past. Because, he said, "by then, when you're in your thirties, nobody asks you if you graduated." His parents, however, didn't know of their son's plan. With just weeks to go before his and Barbara's wedding, his mother and father happened to tell his future in-laws that he hadn't graduated. They considered this important enough that Barbara's father called Tom at work one day and confronted him: "You better tell my daughter, and you better tell her soon," was the message.

And so he did, although when the time came to tell her, at a family get-together, a solemn mood was cast over their apartment. "My parents left early so he could talk to me," Barbara recalled. "He said, 'Barb, there's something I have to tell you.' I thought two things: one, my grandmother (whom I'm very close with) must have died, and my parents couldn't tell me. So they had Tom do it. Or else, I figured Tom had AIDS or some other huge STD.

"When he said, 'Barb, I never graduated college,' I was so relieved. . . . I hugged him hard. It was a huge thing for him not to have told me—but I really was expecting something worse."

When I asked Tom why he kept this a secret, he said that he figured Barbara wouldn't have dated him or taken him seriously at first if she had known. It wasn't for lack of intellect, either, he pointed out. And she agreed with that.

"I remember that he scored higher on his S.A.T. [test] than I did in high school," she said. It just bothered her a great deal, and it still does, that deception will forever be a part of their early history as a couple.

"The problem is," Tom said, in a tone of resignation bordering on disgust, "for the rest of my life I'm going to hear about it. It's like she settled for some guy who didn't finish college."

They reached a compromise: Tom promised to finish his requirements for a degree, which he did in less than a year by going to night school. "He made the choice," Barbara said, although she really meant two choices: not to graduate on time, and then to withhold something from his partner whom he was about to marry. Fortunately for them both, the secret emerged before the wedding and in time for them to address the wounded feelings—on both sides.

Open Spouses, Secret Siblings

Sometimes, even when secrets are exchanged long before the wedding, a couple will spend much of the next year making compromises with forces beyond their control: specifically, with their families. This was the case with Ellie and Steve, twenty-four and twenty-five years old, of St. Louis, who spent months trying to maneuver through a thicket of familial subterfuge. In both cases, of his and her families' secrets, what was at stake wasn't so much their family stability or their marriage. Instead, it was image and inertia, pure but not so simple.

As Steve explained it, some secrets didn't have to be secrets. But in his new marriage, unlike in his family, he wasn't "in charge" of everyone involved. With his wife, he could relax emotionally, let his guard down. "I believe that, in Ellie's family," he said, "they were not raised or taught to deal with situations, to confront them and be up-front and settle the issue—whether it be a family squabble, money problem, or who's going to watch what on TV. And my family is just the opposite.

"The classic example I use is that I have a sister who's gay. And that was extremely difficult for our family to deal with when she went public three years ago," Steve said. "We had many family functions where she and her mate came over—and we do joke about it now—but my parents are still having an incredibly difficult time with it. And that's not to say I still don't have trouble with it myself, but we talk about it, we deal with it, we call each other, we write letters. She has her lifestyle; I have mine." As far as secrets go, he doesn't normally volunteer this information about his family to people he doesn't know well. And neither do his parents, although they are, as he says, working on it.

As for Ellie's family, things got complicated a few years ago when, as she said, "My oldest brother went to jail for three or four months, and nobody around us knew. My parents would go and visit him on weekends, but we [my siblings] couldn't go. We couldn't talk about it."

It turns out this rule of family silence wasn't reserved just for such extraordinary events. Ellie recalled one time when her father and brother had a fistfight and argument about her brother's repeatedly being late for family dinners. They actually left the dining room and went into the next room to fight: "My mother closed the door and made us sit back down at the table and try to eat," Ellie said. "And to this day, I have never seen my parents fight." If they did, they did it in secret. So nowadays, Ellie added, she resents their cloaking behavior, because she feels bad if she needs to argue with Steve loudly or confront him about something. It's as if she's still thinking, "No, don't do it. It's shameful." Or that it should be hidden.

"I resent it," she explained, "because that's not reality. And I've had a problem dealing with it. I mean, when we have a problem, Steve will try to get me to talk about it. But I'm so used to pushing it under, you know, and keeping everything inside."

From Family Secrets to Fears of Infidelity

Early in a marriage, once you've worked through the dark family secrets, as Ellie and Steve have, the most potentially harmful secrets that remain have to do with desires for others or infidelity, however unreal or unlikely that might seem to newlyweds. And most couples therapists would agree that such explosive secrets—ones that involve humiliating betrayal as well as intimate physical acts with others—need to be revealed very carefully if there is to be hope for understanding and possible forgiveness. "The more energy you devote to a secret life and the more guilty you feel about keeping a secret," Doctor Betcher concludes, "the more likely that it is draining your relationship in harmful ways."

Juanita, a twenty-seven-year-old newlywed from Tucson, knows a lot about how relationships can be drained—in a hurry. She was one of a very few new brides I got to know who admitted to having an affair in the first year of marriage; yet she still calls it an "indiscretion," not an affair. She has kept it a secret from her husband, and they are now expecting a baby, in their third year of marriage.

"Marriage can survive a lot," she said. "I really tested it. I would tell Carl I had doubts and felt like I was straying. He learned to be very supportive and to actually talk when I needed him to." When he wouldn't be open with her, which she said was often early on, she felt as if the marriage was empty. "But I kept some things to myself because I didn't want to upset him."

One of those things was Marco, the man with whom she had an affair. "I needed to feel smart, beautiful, educated, and I wasn't getting that [at home]. Along came Marco, and I felt weak around him. He hooked me. It controlled me and I almost wasn't myself. I accepted behavior that I never would have. I almost liked that he told me what to do, and that's not me. I had never seen such machismo in a man except for my dad and brothers—and it seemed more interesting at the time than Carl. I wondered what made him so macho. Plus, he's Hispanic.

"But I never considered leaving Carl for Marco," Juanita said. "I just didn't have enough will to make [the affair] stop. I never meant to be unfaithful. But it's over and it was a test. Carl doesn't know the whole truth and I don't think it's important that he does. What is more important is that we learned we need to communicate to make our marriage work. We survived. It wasn't sexual; I was more out to explore, to learn. We really love each other. If I could erase it, I would."

Without condoning affairs, Betcher and other modern marriage and couples counselors believe that keeping a secret sense of yourself, as one distinct partner, gives you a separateness that may actually help the marriage (though not always). As we've seen, there are healthy and unhealthy secrets. As we've also seen, over time, a secret self may reveal itself when the time is right. Trouble is, the timing is tough to predict and may not be so easy to synchronize between a husband and wife.

"A secret self?" Jennifer, of Phoenix, asked. "I think there are still parts of me that *I* don't know. Like, we just saw a harmonica player recently and I thought, 'That would be fun . . . to play the harmonica.' And then Tim went out and got me one for my birthday. These are things we're finding out about ourselves as we go along."

Secret self or no secret self, these are the kinds of everyday things newlyweds tend to find out right on key. Call them "secrets lite." There's no schedule, there's no hurry.

CHAPTER 5

In-Law Invasions

PROBLEMS AND SOLUTIONS

I call her my monster-in-law.

—Suzette, flight attendant, Delta Air Lines

others-in-law are not evil. Mothers-in-law are not evil. Say it a few more times and you may even believe it. By their nature, no matter the conventional wisdom, mothers-in-law are not evil. What they are, as often as not, is protective, which is a very different thing. Still, for generations mothers-in-law have taken the brunt of the in-law jokes and ribbing. "I call her my monster-in-law," Suzette, twenty-six, a flight attendant from New Orleans, told me on a flight I took returning from a wedding I'd witnessed. "She used to call our house eight or nine times a day during our first year of marriage. Finally I called our pastor and told him I couldn't take this anymore; we got counseling and I finally got an apology from her—a four-page letter."

Why is this the kind of mother-in-law story we're drawn to—and why are these the stories we remember? Largely because mothers-in-law like Suzette's, even if not quite so persistent, have tried time and again to preserve a family order, a sense of tradition that will, by marital law, be no more. And precisely because it will be no more, *someone* has to try to make sure it will be at least a lot like it was before. That someone may be a mother-in-law. Which, if you think about it in a way that most newlyweds don't, is not an easy or an enviable job.

The point here isn't to celebrate or castigate the bullying tactics of toxic parents-in-law but rather to try to explain why so many first-year-marrieds feel anxious or alone when it comes time to make the families mix and they don't mix. Not no way, not no how.

At least, that is, not yet.

Midway in my journey through Newlywedworld, I talked about in-laws one afternoon with Barbara Tober, former editor in chief of *BRIDE'S* magazine. Tober, who worked at the bridal bible for nearly thirty years, mentioned one word repeatedly: "diplomacy." She also talked for a time about negotiations and how important they are in a couple's first year. "The other night," Tober said, "I heard a young wife say to her husband, 'I would move to Australia tomorrow, but you wouldn't leave your mother!' That's what we see all the time." Translation: a lot of acting out when things on the home front haven't been worked out. When our time ran out, Tober presented me with a book, *Wedding Nightmares,* which I smiled at and which I skimmed in the elevator while descending from the *BRIDE'S* thirty-ninth-floor office. On page 145 I spotted a rather apropos "altarcation":

> As the bride walked down the aisle, her soon-to-be mother-in-law rose and yelled, "He's making the biggest mistake of his life!" The bride's cheeks flushed, but still she continued resolutely toward the aisle.
>
> The vows were exchanged, and the couple recessed up the aisle together. "They'll be divorced in six months!" the groom's mother cried out.
>
> The resigned bride explains, "We're different reli-

*gions. On holidays, she calls and tells my husband
they expect him but I'm not invited; leave me in the
car! She even set up a bank account for Mitchell to
use after he divorces me! . . ."[1]*

So it's true. Mother-in-law stories are as prevalent as
bad bridesmaid dresses, and they will probably be
around as long. But monsters-in-law can be tamed, and
fortunately they are the exception. And what you *don't*
hear about in-laws nearly as often as you should, are
stories about sisters- and brothers-in-law and how significant they may turn out to be. You also don't hear
enough about diplomacy; how a spouse can ease a situation diplomatically for the other, even when a rift is
not completely healed.

Siblings-in-Law Surprises

One of my earliest stops along the in-law trail was
Dallas, where I met Cathy and Matt, a newlywed couple in their mid-twenties, who recently had been married in California. While asking them matter-of-factly
about whom they had invited to their wedding and
whom they hadn't, I suddenly felt a whole lotta
squirmin' goin' on:

"Well," Cathy said, laughing softly, "we've had this situation with Matt's siblings that sort of has disrupted our
first year of marriage."

Matt didn't move from his seat, didn't say a word. But
he started shaking his head from side to side.

"You poor thing," Cathy said, "I know."

"You'll get a more balanced perspective from Cathy
on this one," Matt said.

It turned out Cathy was kidding. It wasn't his family
at all that was the problem. It was hers. "Yeah," she

said, "my family, well, my family is kind of like cliquey—my siblings are. And I think from the beginning they felt like Matt didn't fit into the clique. You know, he didn't play golf, or he didn't do this, or didn't do that." So, it seems, they didn't let him *join*—and that's where the trouble began.

For most of the year before her wedding, Cathy was living with her sister and her sister's husband in order to save some money, and she felt she wasn't getting much attention as the soon-to-be-married sister of the family. She felt slighted, taken for granted. "So of course I voiced my opinions to Matt," she said, "and he kind of took it personally—for me. And things kind of started from there." Matt defended his fiancée to his future in-laws, voicing her frustration for her *to them* in a valiant kind of act. So valiant that it backfired.

Later, when Matt would come over to visit Cathy and company, Cathy's brother-in-law simply wouldn't get off the couch to say hello or otherwise recognize Matt's presence. "This guy is a classic fat ass, sit-on-the-sofa, drink-beer-and-watch-TV kind of guy," Matt said. Sort of beats monster-in-law, doesn't it?

"By the time it came around to the wedding," Cathy said, "it's like Matt would say hi to my siblings and that would be it—they never made another effort towards him."

Well, maybe a little effort: "Her brother-in-law called me at work one day," Matt said, "and told me I'm a piece of shit—that's a quote—and lots of other nonsense. It just makes me so angry just to think of him. And as time went on I just got angrier, until I thought about what one of my friends told me. He said that what happened when Cathy and I got married was, we upset the dynamic of her family. And frankly I don't think that they're mature enough—or big enough, respectful enough—to deal with the changes."

Cathy went on to tell me that before she got engaged, her role in the family had always been that she was the wired one, the party animal, the daughter who was dating different guys and always having fun. At family functions, then, she was the entertainer, the one who was drinking and joking and often photographed in people's laps.

"It's more than being the one who was fun," Matt cut in. "You were the one they didn't respect."

"Well, yeah," she said. "I was basically kind of put down or whatever. So I've been trying to change myself over time, and I have changed. And you know, it just so happened that Matt came along at a time when I was changing. And now my family thinks that I've changed *because* of Matt. That he has made me change." And upset the family dynamic.

"Well," Matt said. "It's all true, but in the context of a discussion like this it's kind of oversimplifying it." What he meant to say was that he's glad Cathy changed, but he doesn't take credit for it. She was ready to change long before their marriage but didn't have the support or safety net of a loving partner to help her assert herself; to grow beyond her long-held party-girl family role.

"All of a sudden you're a member of a new clan—like the Hatfields or McCoys."

"One of the larger issues that's involved in the first year of marriage is being inherited by or inheriting a whole new family," says Bryan Brook, Ph.D., a Denver-area couples counselor, psychologist, and author of the book *Design Your Love Life*. "All of a sudden you're a member of a new clan—like the Hatfields or McCoys—and you don't have a choice in the matter." Not only do you give up an amount of freedom when you *couple*—that feeling of "Where am I?" and things you want to do—but a hidden anger often sets in and remains indefinitely, Brook says.

"It's almost as if one is in a sexual fog the first year," he says, bringing sex into the in-law mix (because most newlywed couples won't), "and you begin to realize . . . THIS is NOT what I HAD in MIND! It's very hard to shift your gears into one's definition of who you are. You're into a new social orbit."

Could it be that a new bride—or groom—is embarrassed about appearing *thisclose* or too affectionate in public within this new family setting? Yep. As Penny Bilofsky, Ph.D., points out in *In-Laws/Outlaws,* "No matter how close a family has been, parents have a tendency to feel abandoned when they hear of their child's intention to marry. . . . They are reminded of their own aging as their child takes this next step in the life cycle, and they are also reminded of their child's sexuality."[2]

There's another catch that comes with being in Brook's so-called new social orbit. Oftentimes you are no longer the sun, so to speak, the star of this solar system. You as the new son- or daughter-in-law are forced to share that family spotlight with other family members, people whom you don't know very well, if at all. "Not only may you not be number one anymore," Brook says, "you may not even be number two—or number three. And that's not a pretty picture." The fog thickens.

From many of the male clients he has counseled, Brook (who has been doing this kind of work for twenty years) has heard stories of frustration and confusion that led to tirades and accusations against members of their spouse's family. These husbands are used to being so-called kings of the hill in their homes, or they are used to feeling as if their spouse "had to have their body," to put it in Brook's words. Now it's the Fourth of July family picnic, or Thanksgiving, or a family weekend at the in-laws' home, and things are different. Way different.

"You gunnysack it," Brook says, meaning you basically stuff it and cover it, even if that's not dealing with it. But when you deny the social or sexual compromises you make, you shouldn't go further and pretend they don't matter. Because it's not out of weakness that you're setting those desires and feelings aside. "It's survival," Brook says. "You're trying to justify this decision you made of a lifestyle change." This decision to marry has profound consequences, of course, many of which are beyond your control. Yes, there may be feelings of resentment toward the new family that's yours but not yours, or of being cheated, but believe it: you are not alone in feeling them. After all, you didn't marry your in-laws: you married *into* them. You married a product of their love, one that they are not automatically going to give up to you—the newest member of the family.

In Cathy and Matt's case, Matt believed that members of Cathy's family were not raised or taught to deal with tough situations, confront them openly, and settle the issue at hand, whether it be a family squabble, money, or even who is going to watch what on television. "My family is just the opposite," he said. They like to air things out; they feel they've got to talk their way through problems. Not surprisingly, it's the only style Matt is comfortable with in a family setting.

That's one example of clashing family styles; another emotion to be on the lookout for is resentment. Again, Matt and Cathy offer an example. "I think Cathy's sister just has some incredibly deep-seated, deep-rooted resentment toward her—and me—just from the little snippets I've caught from her and from Cathy," Matt said. Especially when he compares her husband with himself.

According to Cathy, her sister has always been a "type A workaholic," a very put-together accountant, while Cathy described herself as a perennial "type B," who tends to take the path less traveled time and again, often just for the hell of it. "I'm so off-the-line," Cathy said, "and she married somebody like me—her total opposite." At the same time, Cathy married the kind of man her sister probably wishes she had married. "I think she's jealous of that, and she must think [about me]: 'How could *I* have screwed up so much along the way and gotten the right guy?'"

"It sounds conceited in a way," Matt said, "but I've been over to her house and seen it. She'll have one kid in one arm, the other kid she's yelling at, all while stirring a pot with the free hand. And her husband is sitting there—totally out of the picture."

One of the reasons couples are running into more sibling-in-law problems than they used to is age. The later in life a man and women get married—and the average age of marriage is now 24.5 for women and 26.5 for men in the United States—the longer the time there is for sibling ties to grow and bond and weather trying times that the marriage partner will never fully comprehend, largely because he or she simply wasn't around. As a result, there may be jealousy later on when a spouse feels left out of a tight-knit relationship that may have been fostered in a partner's twenties, not necessarily in the teenage years.

There may also be jealousy, Bryan Brook says, when, say, two sisters (one newly married) look forward to spending a Saturday brunch together, *like they've always done,* only now it presents a problem. The other spouse doesn't get it and winds up feeling excluded. "Then there's the competitive side," Brook adds, "when one sister may feel the other has done a little better than she has, partnerwise, or that she's taking better vacations or is making more money.

"If things aren't going well," Brook says, unlike the old days when you'd call your mom or dad, "today you tend to call your sister or brother and say, 'We're having a terrible time! We haven't had sex in two weeks.' Which also can get dicey because the partner may turn around and later say, 'You tell your sister things you don't tell me. That hurts me. Don't you trust me?'" So now you've got secrets problems mixed with in-law strife and evolving sexual behavior within a brand-new marriage. It's a potent mix.

On the whole, sisters-in-law are not evil. Brothers-in-law are not evil. Say it until you believe it . . . but they can be wicked. Whenever there's unfinished business between siblings, according to Brook, you can count on that being stirred up when a marriage partner comes into a family. A newly wedded couple should be entitled to set boundaries so that they maintain their individual identities, their identity as a couple, and, as they wish, their identities as part of their family of origin.

In-Laws and Out-Law Behavior

"Within every new family, there are so many issues of 'intentional togetherness,'" Brook says. None, perhaps, is as highly charged as holiday time, but you probably know that already. What you may not know is why that is so. It turns out that holiday pressures go way beyond shopping and who's cooking what and what time to show up—they have to do with exaggerated feelings. "Because we're *supposed* to feel more love" during certain times or days of the year, Brook explains, the tension that would already be apparent, say, on any given nonholiday Tuesday in July is heightened on holidays. And then, if the love doesn't magically multiply—more, more—on cue, a couple may wonder, "What's wrong with this picture?" when there may not be anything wrong at all.

Toward the end of my interview with Matt and Cathy, I reassured them that as far as I, an unshy amateur psychologist, could tell, their in-law problems were par for the dysfunctional course. I even said Cathy's family was probably seen as "ideal" because at least they were a family that was intact: never mind that they couldn't stand up and really talk among themselves about issues that matter. They would forever save them for later.

"Matt and I know we have problems," Cathy said, "and he will have to try to get me to talk about them. I'm so used to pushing it under and keeping everything inside. But I'm still back in my world where I have this perfect little ending in my mind. Since we got married, it's made me realize how much my past affects the way I deal with things now." Or in some cases, how she doesn't deal with things.

It's interesting, too, that Cathy focuses on and uses the word "reality" when discussing her past role models. As Maggie Scarf points out in *Intimate Partners,* when couples marry, they must set about redefining themselves in line with their new visions of themselves and in line with their *different* definitions of reality. This, as you might expect, does not happen neatly in the first week or month of marriage. Especially when you've got in-laws mixed into the mélange.

"Each member of the pair," Scarf writes, "has . . . come into the marriage with a different autobiography; the specific family cultures from which they spring have impressed certain ideas and beliefs into their psyches. . . . The major struggle, in the early phase of marriage, is about what the themes of their new, jointly scripted scenario will be."[3] The minor struggles, meanwhile, are the day-to-day dealings about casting aside parts of the past and deciding what you call your

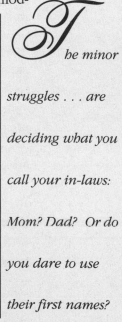

The minor struggles . . . are deciding what you call your in-laws: Mom? Dad? Or do you dare to use their first names?

in-laws: Mom? Dad? Or do you dare to use their first names? The unofficial rule: If you're comfortable enough to ask them, chances are you'll be able to call them Mom or Dad.

"Well," Matt said, "her parents are alert to some of these [bigger] things now, but in their own way they mean very well, and that means a lot to me. They really did made me feel welcome."

"I want my family to be just as enjoyable as his," Cathy said, "but it turns out we're both so much more relaxed around his family. Which is weird for me, because you know my family's always been the 'good' family, you know, in the neighborhood."

Holiday Hassles and More

To be sure, newlyweds will always compare parents-in-law. It's a rite and a sport. And Mark and Leesa, a newly married Atlanta couple, stepped right up to play.

"To be quite frank," Mark told me, "my mom is an eccentric kind of person who I think is an incredible businesswoman who's also eccentric. She has her own views on life but also on the bottom line. So in our families, in-laws don't get along. In the classic sense it's probably like most people who believe what they see about [married] couples when they watch TV."

Their first rule of in-law renegotiation? "We've already agreed on it," Mark, a lawyer, said. "We did it for the first year—went to the folks for the holidays; maybe next year, too, and that's that. From then on it's going to be our own tradition, and if people want to be with us on Christmas, they can come to our house.

"We'll still go celebrate, go to people's houses and stuff," Mark added. "We're not saying we won't—we're just saying that our traditions will become fundamentally first. They will be the first things we'll do on holidays."

This last year was especially hard on Leesa and Mark, because while Leesa's family always gathers in Memphis every Thanksgiving, this time she couldn't join them: her work as an industrial designer got in the way. And it's a holiday, Leesa said, "that for my family, basically, sets up our year."

"And the boys get to go duck hunting at the best duck-hunting spot in the country," Mark said. He sounded genuinely disappointed to have missed that part of the in-law experience. They're not all bad, you know.

"I was on the verge of 'I'll fly out for the night, I'll just go and see them on Thanksgiving, one night and I'll fly back,'" Leesa said. "And it got to the point where we had to say no, we don't have the money to do that. So we decided, let's make our own tradition when we can't go to Memphis. We ended up going to his mom's house on Thanksgiving," Leesa said. "Which was fine, but during the day we *tried* to set up a Christmas. We had a big breakfast and mimosas and set up our Christmas tree and did all our Christmas decorating stuff. We tried so hard our first year just to do our own thing so I wouldn't be so depressed."

Depression isn't exactly the word that comes to mind when Linda, thirty-two, a waitress, thinks about holidays and her twenty-four-year-old husband, Tim's, family. Bewilderment maybe, but not depression. "They're okay," she said. "I wish that I could like them better, though. I really want to, but they just irritate the shit out of me. I don't have patience for them. Sometimes," she said, "I feel like they say things about me, even if I can't put my finger on it. Tim says it's in my head, but I think they say things in jabs—like about money. They'll say: 'You and Linda are always goofing off and going bungee jumping or skydiving or doing these things,' and it's like, 'That must cost . . . whatever!' Then they look at me like I'm the one responsible for it."

Of course she isn't the *only* one responsible for the "irresponsible" spending, but she will have to take the heat for it because, well, "Tim was never like that before with *his* money." It makes sense, too, when you look at it from his parents' perspective—even if that isn't—or doesn't seem—fair to Linda. To be precise, it's the tone of the thought that irritates her to no end.

"Tim's father thinks the whole world's going to come to an end," she explained from her San Jose, California, home, "and whoever doesn't have money is going to die." Finally, she asked her husband to intervene in this uncomfortable little war, and he did. Tim told his dad, asked him actually, to let him and Linda work out their money matters by themselves. Their father-in-law problem, fortunately, dissipated.

Unfortunately, they also had a mother-in-law problem in their first year of marriage—his. According to Linda, "My mom makes him very uptight. But then again, my mom makes me uptight. I can barely be in a room with her for more than ten minutes before I want to kill her. (I've always been like that—we both have such strong personalities.) My mom is very rude to Tim sometimes, and other times she goes out of her way to be so nice to him that it throws him for a loop. I don't know if she thinks she's being rude; my mom's always like that to people."

The saving grace for Tim in this relationship is the deep-seated feelings he knows she has for both Linda and him, even if she won't always express them. On their wedding day, in fact, Linda's mother told her she was "so genuinely happy" that Linda was marrying Tim and that it was clear to her that her daughter was deeply in love.

With some in-law puzzles already solved, the biggest problems that remain in the early stages of Tim and Linda's marriage are their holiday madcap races around the state. "Both our parents are divorced and remarried," Linda said. "We have four sets, plus grand-parents. So what we're trying to do now is . . . Thanks-giving at one family's, Christmas at another, and another. But this last Christmas it just got too hectic. Tim and I spent Christmas morning with just us open-ing presents—and then Tim went to his mom's, and then he went to his dad's. Meanwhile, I spent time with my family, and my dad came over on Christmas eve."

In short, they spent a lot of Christmas day apart from each other.

"We kind of split up now on holidays," Linda said, "because I just love holidays with my family because we have so much fun. And his family, to me, I'm bored sick; it's like seven to eight hours of talking about news. Whereas, at our house, we don't talk about all the famines and the world coming to an end and vio-lence and money. We talk about funny things, we talk about, oh, 'I did this the other day,' and play jokes on each other. And his family's just so much more serious. They'll worry about everything."

No More Worries? or Just Fewer of Them?

One thing Linda doesn't worry about anymore is how to justify her and Tim's choices how to do Christ-mas. This is a change, and a welcome one. The first time they did their madcap holiday rounds (while en-gaged), it seems Tim's father actually called Linda and told her that "never in a million years" would he be without *his* bride on Christmas. "And I said, 'Well, Dan, you're not me. And besides, you probably don't have four sets of parents to go see.'"

"Families are so highly at risk in our culture," says therapist Brook. "There are so many factors pulling them apart. I think only one in four families now fits the standard description of a nuclear family."

"I get so sick to my stomach knowing that I have to go to his family's house," Linda said. "I mean, I have to be told a month ahead of time, just so I can plan and get in the mood to go over there. I know this sounds really terrible, but I get stoned before I go there.

"Then I can just sit there," she said, "and just go, 'Oh shit!' One night his family sat around the fireplace and sang while Tim's brother was playing, 'Michael Row Your Boat Ashore' and 'Cum-ba-ya'—that kind of music. And Grandma was playing the tambourine, and everybody was holding hands. They were so serious!"

This is not what sing-along means in the culture of Linda and sister Rita and their mom. "I mean," Linda says, "with my family, we get out, we turn on the karaoke machine, and we make fun of my mom doing country western dancing. That kind of stuff. Everything we do is on a funnier note than their family. I guess they just have a stricter moral upbringing." But how does she *really* feel? "I just think they're really boring," she said, playing along.

For his part, Tim wishes that Linda would make an effort to go along with his family's discussions and activities on the few days that she is there. Because, as he puts it, he makes a big effort at *her* mother's house. And going along would, obviously, make things easier for him. You see, "Tim's also the baby of the family; Tim put himself through school; and Tim is their life," she says. "Tim and his dad talk to each other at least five times a week on the phone. I think that they think I've taken their son from them, because he doesn't go over there as much. Before we got married, Tim was over there at least once a week for dinner, and I mean we just don't do that anymore."

Could it be that Linda, the big talker and ever confident wife, might feel a little leftover resentment here?

"Maybe," she said, "because I always felt like I was trying to get my dad and mom's approval for everything—when I felt I was doing so much better than the rest of my brothers and sisters in life. And to this day I still feel like my mom was so much harder on me than everybody. And I still don't get the respect I deserve. So maybe deep down it may be that I'm a little jealous of it." That's two "may-be's" in one answer. That's another way of saying she's still adjusting to sharing her husband and feeling detached from some of his greatest attachments.

As is pretty evident here, you can't count on resolving in-law problems in a swift and tidy manner. One reason is, there is simply so much at stake for each of the parties involved. Remembering Cathy and Matt can be instructive: although their siblings-in-law were big-time trouble, the parents-in-law were fine. Matt told me, in fact, "I particularly like Cathy's dad. He's a very solid, respectable, down-to-earth guy with a good sense of humor."

This surprised Matt at first because Cathy's father is well-off financially, with a country club membership and friends in the right kinds of places. Matt expected a different sort of swagger than the one he saw when he met him. "When I went to ask his permission to marry Cathy," Matt said, "I thought it was funny, because we met up halfway on the road. I was in the [navy] reserves at the time, and I had to take part in a drill near his home. So we arranged to meet at this Hilton—in a bar.

"I got to the word 'marry,' and that was all I got out.

The next thing I knew he was jumpin' all over me. And I'm thinking," Matt said, "'This doesn't look good—there's some older man hugging this younger guy in uniform.' . . . But I really like her dad; and her parents make me feel welcome."

I asked them, finally, if there was any irony in the details of the arrangement Matt had made with Cathy's father way back when.

"How's that?" Matt asked.

"How you met *halfway*," I said.

"Yeah?" Cathy said.

"Yeah," Matt said.

It was, to be sure, not a bad compromise. And it won't be the last one.

CHAPTER 6

Just-Married Sex

THE JOY, THE FEARS, HOW IT REALLY FEELS

*Simultaneous orgasms are not common—
and, in fact, probably not worth striving for.
If by chance they happen, fine.*

—*The Kinsey Institute New Report on Sex, 1990*

orget the silken lingerie. Hold the candles. Unplug the vibrator. Leave the whipped cream in the refrigerator—at least for now. As newlywed lovers, the first thing you can do to actually improve your sex life throughout your first year is . . . relax. For as the famed Kinsey Institute for Sex Research preaches at the head of this chapter, such feats as simultaneous orgasms and erotic acrobatics are often overrated. Of course, some of us also believe it is way better than "fine" to experience simultaneous orgasms every once in a while. But too many of us will find ourselves running into trouble in bed if we try too hard too often for the elusive two-at-once. After all, as the minister, priest, or rabbi says, the point is to have and to hold—not simultaneously explode.

What Is "Normal," Anyway?

Apparently, that point is not always clearly understood. Without a lot of warning, millions of unwary newlyweds stumble into problems that involve sex and intimacy in their first married year. They've heard the tale about putting a bean in the jar every time they have sex during their first year of marriage: how, supposedly, if they take one out every time they have sex after their first anniversary on, the jar will never be empty. But that's old news. Here and now, couples still expect far too much. Therapist Terry Real says newlyweds are often confused about their sex lives because they aren't sure whether theirs is normal or fulfilling enough. Ease up, he advises. Take some of the pressure about sex away from your first-year concerns. After all, he says, "Do you expect to be completely fulfilled by your work all the time?" Well, no. It's the same with sex—or it ought to be. Besides, one recent national survey of 1,049 adults found that 67 percent of married people were happy with their sex lives, while only 45 percent of unmarried adults said they were happy with theirs.[1] So, compared with singles, even though married folks may feel *better* about their sex lives, a third of them still say they aren't satisfied with the way things are going in bed.

In an interview setting, Real is engaging and frank when he talks about sex, love, and marriage. He wants newlyweds to know The Truth. "By and large, romance is a crock," he says. "By and large, it's great in the audition phase of a relationship, and it can last into the commitment phase and the honeymoon phase, but it almost always ends after the first child is born." Real goes on to explain that if a couple feels their relationship is supposed to be *based* in romance, it will invariably lead to feelings of inadequacy and shame. In fact, he believes that misconception to be "one of the guilty secrets we carry around along with the couple next door."

To be sure, sex is an important part of marriage. But so is one's career; so are one's families, friends, and

other interests. Together all these daily life experiences
bring fulfillment to a couple that transcends each one
individually. All of which makes sense. Why, then, do
we persist in demanding so much from our sexual
selves, *especially* so early on in marriage? For starters, it
helps to remember that sex, as a pleasure, is seen as
something you can start to change, to some degree, almost immediately. You could do something about it
tonight—or tomorrow morning. (And hopefully for the
better.) It's a different story when it comes to your in-
laws or finances. In many cases, one of the first questions about sex to arise is: why isn't there as much sex
going on ten months after the wedding as there was just
ten days after?

Which brings up a related question: as great as it can
be, is so-called honeymoon sex the standard to aim
for?

One February day, I went to visit a newly wedded
bride in the Bible Belt city of Tulsa, Oklahoma, who
had told me in confidence some months earlier that
she thought a newlywed couple should have sex "often." How often, I asked. Ten times a week was her re-
ply. *Ten* times a week. What Bible Belt? I thought. Then
I wondered if it was perhaps my age (mid-thirties) that
made me envious of this revelation, for she and her
husband (an accountant!) were in their early twenties.
Or maybe it was that once God and clergy unite a couple in marriage in this part of the country, all bets are
off with sexual restraint, and all fun is on. Ten times indeed . . . long after the honeymoon photos have been
developed and duly mounted.

In *Sex in America,* a scholarly and widely cited study
of more than 3,400 adults aged eighteen to fifty-nine,
conducted by University of Chicago researchers in the
early 1990s, two key findings emerged. First, it was reported that married people have more sex than those

who are single—41 percent of married couples have
sex twice a week or more, compared with only 23 percent of singles. That makes sense. In these times sex
between near-strangers and singles doesn't occur
nearly as often as it did in the freewheeling 1970s.
When it came to more frequent sexual encounters,
however, things evened out: only 7 percent of married
people and 7 percent of singles told the researchers in
interviews that they had sex four or more times a
week.[2] So maybe ten times a week isn't normal for
most marrieds, but for those who *just* got married, it
might not be that unusual. After all, it's brand new.

For another view, I asked Carol, a thirty-year-old from
outside of Baltimore, about her take on early marital re-
lations. "The best sex I ever had was the Saturday
evening *before* my wedding," she answered. "It was by
far the sweetest, most tender, most full of love." As Carol
went on to describe it, this sex wasn't exactly wild. Or
crazy. In fact, it was the opposite of what so many people think honeymoon-phase sex is going to be.

What happened was, Carol and her fiancé had just
endured a long commuter-relationship period because
of their jobs, and finally this stretch was over: no more
frantic, quick-grab sessions on the couch on the way to
catch a cab to the airport, no more late-night cooing
over the long distance lines (after the rates had
dropped). To Carol, pleasure and time—expanses of
it—were now front and center. "We were just that
happy," she said. "Pete and I had spent the day buying
clothes—I got my trousseau from the Gap! It was about
seven o'clock, and we had just ordered his tux for the
rehearsal dinner. We lay down to take a nap, and it
blossomed into this half hour of heaven. It was so
sweet and tender . . . so full of love. Neither of us was
working at the time; we were just thinking about getting married and being happy. A friend of mine came

over afterwards and she *knew*. She teased me, saying, 'Go brush your hair!' Basically, I had sex hair."

Carol may be coy at times, but she is not what you would call a shy bride. In telling me about sex, sex hair, and early newlywed life, she openly mentioned feelings she won't soon forget—when, during sex, she would "break out in a cold sweat—literally. I would start shaking, shuddering all over my body before we made love." She went on to talk about a time, well before her first anniversary, when she experimented with pain and pleasure. By that she meant "not blood and whips of course, but pinching and biting. Then we'd ask each other, 'Does that hurt?' or, 'Does that feel good?'"

If you consider what counselor Real says about the commitment and honeymoon phases of romance and love in a relationship, you could classify Carol's comments as falling within the boundaries of both phases. All these feelings, and they hadn't even eased out of the honeymoon phase yet (although they were about to do so).

The point I found most compelling about her, though, was that the best sex she ever had was a week before her wedding, not right after it, as is the case with so many other couples and their newlywed experiences. In fact, sometime in the first few months after her wedding, Carol had a stark, painful realization. The sex in her marriage "dropped off radically," she admitted. "We had our honeymoon, but then, exactly a month after the perfect sex, he wouldn't touch me. *One month* after. . . . He said, 'I can see sex is going to be a problem,' because he thought I wanted it too much."

"Sure," Betsy, thirty-six, of Fort Atkinson, Wisconsin, told me, it's important for a couple to have sex in the first year of marriage "so they can remember good times after real life sets in. But if it's a good marriage [hers was three years strong when she spoke], the first-year sex comes back like the tide—in some ways better! There's more comfort; you know the person better. Later, when the kids are older and people are not at risk of pregnancy, sex can still be better—I've heard and read."

If Carol had heard about or read the May 1994 issue of *Glamour* magazine, she would have seen an article that asked: "Is it true that after the honeymoon, you never have sex again?" She would have focused on every word.

"Before we got married it was three times a day, in every room in the house," Carol said, sounding as if that was ten years ago, not one and a half. "It used to be, at breakfast, he'd put me up on the counter and there we'd go. Then after we got married, it was three times a *week,* which even dwindled down to one time a week.

"The first-year-of-marriage shit winds up killing your sex drive—for men I guess," Carol told me sadly. "I guess I was using that [sex] to hold on to things. I'd say to myself, 'I know he loves me because he just made love to me.'" One has to wonder whether Carol's expectations were out of whack or whether there weren't, as we'll see later, other issues complicating the mix.

Lauren, thirty-one, from northern California, also felt a change in her and her husband's sexual habits almost before she knew it, easily before all the wedding gifts had arrived. "It was all the *time* the first year we were together," she said. "I mean, four times a day was not unlikely for us. Now, I would say it's three times a week, tops, and most likely once or twice. But," she allowed, "a lot of that also has to do with [the fact that] I went off the birth control pill and so I'm not as spontaneous anymore." As a result, when Lauren and her husband, Ron, didn't have a condom or some other means

"Is it true that after the honeymoon, you never have sex again?"

of birth control handy, she felt uncomfortable. And un-
excited. To this day, she still doesn't like having to feel
so *responsible* about having sex. "Before," she said, "it
might be that we'd be on a picnic somewhere and have
sex right there—no biggie!—yet it was a very passionate thing. Whereas I would never do that now." Contra-
ception can be a mood killer when real life gets in the
way of the heat of the moment.

Basically, Lauren and Ron discovered by themselves
what thousands of couples discover only after seeing a
counselor of some kind: that sexual dry spells occur in
most every intimate relationship. "The Sexual Sahara" is how Cleveland-area sex therapist and author Sherry Lehman describes
it. While many therapists say that *all* relationships move from the passionate to the
comfortable after a while, Lehman feels it
is also not unrealistic to expect one's marriage to remain fulfilling and exciting. "It is
possible, but it requires a lot of work," she
says in *It Was Better in the Backseat: How
to Recharge Your Sex Life.*[3] And the work
starts not with sex toys or lingerie but with understanding and trust.

Sexual dry spells occur in most every intimate relationship.

"You should be able to touch yourself in front of
your partner," advises sex educator Suzi Landolphi, author of *Hot, Sexy and Safer.* If you happen to be too
shy or ashamed to touch your own body and help stim-
ulate yourself sexually, then you aren't ready for the intimate sharing that is needed for intercourse. As
Landolphi describes it, intercourse is a true show-and-
tell. One person needs to say, "Hey, let's try *this.*"

Carol, for one, is trying to understand. "A male friend
of mine once said, 'Fucking is boring. It's everything
else that goes with it that's interesting.' That's what hap-

pens after you're married," she said. "You do A, B, C, and D [in bed], and it gets to the point where you'd rather watch the evening news and *learn* something. In our case it went from me making breakfast and him jumping my bones down to once a week—on Sunday.

"On the other hand," Carol added, "now that we're married, we let more naughty things come through."

What is naughty in bed to one couple, of course, may be benign to another and licentious to still another. For example, in the movie, *Sirens*, which starred Hugh Grant, Tara FitzGerald, Sam Neill and Elle Macpherson, Grant and FitzGerald played a staid, recently married clergyman and wife whose sensibility and sensuality were called into question when they visited an artist's estate where nudity and sexuality were celebrated. After the Grant character witnessed his wife cavorting with apparently bisexual, skinny-dipping female portrait models, he knew something was wrong.

"One person needs to say, "Hey, let's try this . . ."

"Piglet, you all right?" he asked.

"I think we should talk," she answered.

"Right you are," he said. "What's wrong?"

"Ever since we got here, ah . . . oh . . ."

Then she stopped. She seemed ready to tell him about the strange forces swirling about her, or about a sexual awakening she felt amidst all this body worship, or perhaps she was about to confess her dalliance with the sirens. He cut her off.

"Now you see," Grant's character said. "I think, I think some things are best left unsaid . . ."

"[But] that means we'll always be strangers."

"No, not really—only small parts of us . . . ," he said. "I think it's good to have a few secrets . . . That way, in fifty years, we'll still be able to surprise each other."

"Perhaps you're right," his wife said.

From Fear of Infidelity to Better Sex

There are times, of course, when you don't want your partner to "say it" or "do it." For instance, when Don, forty-two, a screenwriter from Los Angeles, "finally" got married, he was more worried about his sex life breaking down than having to build it up again. "The first year was a huge adjustment," he said. "I remember when we first got married and my wife had to go on location for two and a half months. I had never been monogamous in my life, and I figured I'd better cover my bases here." In other words, he thought he should prepare his wife in case *either* of them should happen to stray, to cheat on one another, during their separation. Unhealthy as this may sound to outsiders, it turned out better for the two of them than many might have expected.

"I said to her, 'You know, if you're out one night and you have . . . you know, if you're feeling needy or whatever and you *do* something, I don't want to know about it,'" Don said. "I was 'pre-forgiving' her for an infidelity, because what I was *really* doing was protecting me. Because I figured, 'Well, I'm definitely going to fuck around, because I've never been in a monogamous relationship in my life.' I mean, I had never been married or anything."

When I asked whether Don's wife caught on to his suave presentation, he didn't answer directly. "She just looked at me, like, 'What the hell are you *talking* about?'" But in reality Don was more jealous of his new wife's easy camaraderie on the job with coworkers of both sexes than he was concerned about his own unfulfilled sexual impulses. He called her repeatedly, checking up on her, almost to annoyance. "It was sort of like a little marital dance we did with each other," he said, full well knowing it was a clumsy two-step. "We still laugh about it," he added. It wasn't phone sex exactly; more like phone flirting. This is also an example of a couple that may be advanced in years when it comes to age of marriage—his early forties and her mid-thirties—but neither were they sexually mature as a couple, at least not yet.

Because Don had sounded a rather urgent early warning about sexual urges and fears of infidelity, I asked therapist Real about them. I wondered whether what you do sexually in your first year of marriage will somehow dictate the patterns of how your sex life will ultimately unfold.

"People love to refer to that early phase [of marriage] as if that's what the relationship is supposed to be like," he says, pointing out there are important misconceptions here, too. "The early phase of a relationship is what I call the nose-to-nose phase. It's a very narcissistic phase; it's an *in-love* phase. It's a phase when the couple is staying up till three o'clock in the morning. It used to be they'd be smoking cigarettes, talking. We don't do that anymore—now it's herbal tea." He laughs. "And you know there's a lot of sex, but it's not just sex."

In this phase of a relationship, Real adds, you'll also find a lot of emotional profundity. "You have made a vow to each other, and there's that whole energy—the same energy that's captured in an affair." He further explains that this energy is erotic, intense, and serves to prove to both of you that you really are fascinated with each other. It's the kind of feeling that can reach a point where, as viewed from the outside, a couple in the throes are disgusting to be around on certain days. You know, all goo-goo eyed.

This is all well and good, to a point. "But a healthy couple moves out of that phase in fairly short order," Real says. "It could be a few weeks, could be a few years. But sooner or later if they're healthy they move from that nose-to-nose energy to what I call a side-by-side energy." It's worth noting that in talking about the cooling of sexual feelings, Real refers to a decidedly nonsexual position: side by side. And what's different about this side-by-side phase is that the couple's main focus shifts—away from just them and then toward the life that they're living. They buy a house, start new careers, have kids. They start being about the things they're building together. And, according to Real, that energy is a much more routine, domestic, *less erotic, less fascinated, less intense* kind of energy. Still, it's healthy.

In the city known as the capital of Texas—Austin—I came upon a newlywed, Lucia, who at forty, has been through the nose-to-nose phase (with two husbands) and who seems to be preparing for the side-by-side. (At least as far as the question of fidelity goes.) I told her about the statistics estimating half of all married men have sex with other partners and that the rate is becoming the same for women. Then I asked her if she could *envision* a case in which a newlywed has an affair and the marriage survives. "Yes," she said. "It must work for some people since it is so common." Maybe she has a more realistic view of sex and marriage than most newlyweds, having had more experience than the average bride of twenty-five, but then again, maybe she was being both unrealistic and cavalier about the vows she recently had taken.

It turns out Lucia's husband, Craig, thirty-three, did not agree with his wife of ten months. "To tell the truth," he said, he couldn't imagine an instance where a marriage could survive this kind of breach. "Love means trust," he explained, not leaving a lot of room for error. "Fidelity is part of the foundation for marriage. This applies to both men and women!"

As for other husbands' views, "If you think hot rock-'n'-roll kind of sex is the be-all and end-all of the relationship, your marriage won't last," said one husband who was quoted in the *Glamour* article mentioned earlier. "Once you're married, you lose that thrill of first contact, sure—but my wife and I have more fun now, because it's more relaxed. You don't lower your expectations—you become more complete."[4]

And as for more scientific proof for this change, it isn't plentiful, but it's out there. In the stacks of the Harvard University library, for instance, you can find an issue of the *Journal of Nonverbal Behavior,* in which a study reported that "men initiated touch significantly more in casual romantic relationships, but women initiated touch more in married relationships."[5] Maybe that's why some married men feel as if they don't have the same lust they used to carry around in their singlehood.

"I always wanted to write a book called *What Nobody Will Tell You About Marriage—More Fights and Less Sex Than You Ever Dreamed Possible,"* Real likes to say. He himself has been married once and divorced.

Top Ten Things About Newlywed Sex

One way to put newlywed sex in perspective is to get out pencil and paper and make a list. Which I asked ten eager newlyweds to do—anonymously. Here are some of the more telling things that emerged about what is pretty great about sex in early married life.

With apologies to "The Late Show with David Letter-man," it should be noted that in this top ten honesty counts more than humor.

10. Not having to worry so much if the rubber breaks.
9. Saturday mornings in bed that turn into after-noons—not going out till dinner . . .
8. Being able to turn the lights on.
7. No more STDs.
6. Trying out every room in our house.
5. Not having to try to impress the person I'm with with my sexual prowess.
4. Having—and getting—oral sex . . . at *any* time of the month.
3. Finally trying a fantasy.
2. Having a quickie before work . . . and saying we'll finish later.

And the number one best thing about sex in the first year of marriage is . . .

1. No more faking!!!

How and When Desire Differs

When it comes to sexual desire in marriage, as unique as each couple may be, there is one basic dif-ference between men and women, according to Pep-per Schwartz, Ph.D., professor of sociology at the University of Washington and author of the book *Peer Marriage.* As a sociologist with a keen interest in sexu-ality, Schwartz believes that wives, on average, are more apt to "let their sex life slide" than men are be-cause women have a wider variety of means with which to satisfy their needs for intimacy: talking with women friends; touching, hugging, or breastfeeding their children; or perhaps reliving past experiences. Meanwhile, wives have told Schwartz that the only time many husbands show themselves "to be emotionally needy is during sex." It is the only time they allow themselves to be vulnerable.[6] True (and controversial) as this might be, this doesn't mean men don't enjoy sex as much as women. Nor does it necessarily mean that they use it for the wrong reasons. It means only that as time goes on their need for it, as far as intimacy is concerned, won't likely match their wives'.

In answer to Schwartz's observations, one Phoenix newlywed, Sarah, twenty-eight, told me she is indeed able to look to her past to fulfill some of her present needs for intimacy. For instance, when she was in college, she remembers giving in to her boyfriends' requests for oral sex—cunnilingus, to be specific—even though she didn't like it all that much. "A lot of them liked doing that, and I'd say, 'Fine,' and sometimes, you know, I'd act like I was really enjoying it," she said. "It's not that I wasn't enjoying it at all. It's just that I never got past the feeling that it was just okay. I guess I just figured I was incapable of orgasm." Meanwhile, she explained, "It was always really exciting—just to get them off [sexually] and to be with a different person."

These days she is with one person, her husband, Ed, with whom she doesn't have to pretend to have an orgasm. And fortunately, she has found other ways to achieve intimacy without simply succumbing to her partner's wishes. She is quite willing and able, for example, to direct her husband's hands, mouth, and penis to areas of her body that elicit some rather powerful orgasms. The lessons of her past still arise now and then, but they are safely in the past. "I never had an orgasm until I was twenty, even though I had slept with a lot of people," she said. Needless to say, the last year of married life has been quite different. She has—and Terry Real would be pleased to hear this—learned to relax.

"When I was younger," Sarah said of her sexual experiences, "I had this [fear] where I would never take my underwear off—unless it was totally dark. And you know, as you get older, you don't mind that."

Another newlywed, Donna, thirty, from West Virginia, found, "I had no basis to believe this, but I did think there was something in marriage that would make us better lovers. . . . I was glad I was marrying a man who had more experience than I had. I was relieved. I thought I could show him when I felt scared sexually or that he would know when one of us was too busy trying to please the other person in bed." Unlike most of the other women interviewed in these pages, however, Donna got divorced within three years. She went on to explain:

"After James and I separated, I realized that I was more experienced sexually than my 'experienced' husband. He'd been *fucking,* as far as I was concerned. He had his numbers, but there was no intimacy. What he thought was wild was location—*where* he did it. But I realized that I was much more comfortable with my body than he was with his. He couldn't face the fact that I had undergone a dramatic transformation sexually, at twenty-three or twenty-four, before we were married. I was dishonest with myself, rather than letting him know I was lonely, unhappy, and disinterested in sex. By our first anniversary, I knew we weren't going to make it." Although Donna doesn't blame the lack of sexual intimacy for causing her marriage to break apart, she knows it was a major factor leading to their divorce.

"It's not unusual for men to misperceive what really influences women's sexual drives," says Jennifer Knopf, Ph.D., director of the sex and marital therapy program at Northwestern University in Chicago. "In general there is too much focus on techniques. What I think needs to be followed up on is the *relationship atmosphere.*" In other words a woman or a man has to be comfortable before he or she can be aroused.

On the male side of the equation, from the honeymoon on, countless husbands have had to deal with the embarrassing occurrence of performance anxiety: when they wanted to make love but simply couldn't get an erection. Thus, intercourse becomes impossible. This problem can easily lead to loss of desire, especially when it goes unacknowledged. When performance anxiety strikes (and it does happen to most men, at least occasionally), they can make matters better by dwelling temporarily on the other aspects of lovemaking, like mutual massage. Prominent sex therapist Bernie Zilbergeld, Ph.D., of Oakland, California, for one, goes so far as to extol the virtues of couples who are able to enjoy the "pleasures of a soft penis." Many men are "horrified" at the prospect of having a partner touch their unerect penis, he says. "They believe it should be hard before she touches it or, at the very least . . . as soon as she touches it. That's the fantasy."[7] I'll admit I was somewhat embarrassed when I, as a reporter, asked Zilbergeld to elaborate about these pleasures, because they didn't sound, well, normal. But he has apparently explained this so often that when he did so again, he sounded like a weathercaster zipping through the five-day forecast at the end of the eleven o'clock news. To put it briefly, he said men haven't been taught that having a soft penis is manly. This could pose extra problems early in a marriage, when virility is supposed to be at its peak.

Another thought to keep in mind, according to Terry

Nerves may cause him to seek sex when all he really wants is reassurance.

Real, is that if a husband is nervous because he has to make a presentation or give a big speech at work the next day, it might or might not cause performance anxiety. His nerves may cause him to seek sex when all he *really* wants is reassurance or some support from his partner. It's just that he might find it easier to reach out for that support under the covers late at night rather than in the kitchen, face-to-face, a mere hour and a half after work. He may want to talk, Real says, "but what he knows to do is grab her in bed."

Zilbergeld and Real's point—of letting your guard down and changing your expectations—is well-taken. Since so many people enter marriage today more sexually experienced than their cohorts of thirty years ago, they expect more from the partners they've vowed to make love with exclusively for the rest of their lives. This is due in part to their appetites having been whetted in ways that past generations of newlyweds' appetites hadn't.

At the same time, today's newlyweds likely have had intercourse in an era in which the specter of herpes, HIV/AIDS, and other sexually transmitted diseases has caused fear and has actually inhibited many a partner's sense of sexual freedom. At an age when they might be expected to be at their wildest, they were forced to associate unprotected intercourse with the possibility of contracting a deadly disease. This is especially true among young women, when you consider that 37 percent of the women infected with AIDS in the United States in the early 1990s contracted the disease through heterosexual intercourse, whereas only 3 percent of men contracted it that way. Modern husbands and wives, it seems, have faced some formidable barriers and intimidation when it comes to their sexual development as adults, no matter how free society may appear to be in terms of sex.

Inevitably, it seems, when fear associated with an activity like intercourse is rampant, couples will tend to forsake wildness for safety, and something may get lost along the way. The editors of *New York* magazine put it rather simply on the cover of their March 6, 1995, issue: On a stark, 1950s type black-and-white photograph of a young husband and wife in close embrace, they superimposed the words "Why Nobody Cheats Anymore." On the other hand, after dealing with anxieties, fears, and threats of disease, marriage may be just the arrangement needed to finally free a spouse or a couple from feelings of repression about sex.

Sexual Games, Toys, and Variety

There are other ways, of course, for couples to break free of sexual fears and patterns, but they aren't always easy to employ in the first few months after the honeymoon. Some are easy enough to get hold of, like sexy videotapes, lingerie, vibrators, dildos, or glow-in-the-dark condoms. Others are more elusive. Henry James Borys reveals in *The Way of Marriage* that one of the ways he and his wife, Susan, kept their sex life bright during some stormy days of their early married years was to make love while trying *not* to have orgasms. This is not unheard of, to be sure, in some of the Eastern religious practices that grew out of the Tao, or in India, where a spiritual technique known as Tantric sex (big on the naked hugging, holding, and breathing) is widely practiced.

Borys says his and his wife's goal was not merely birth control but a way of being connected physically that was perhaps *more* intimate than coming. "We have found that making love without the expectation of an orgasm eliminates a subtle level of self-absorption in our sex."

Vicki Hufnagel, M.D., gynecologist, surgeon, and women's health advocate from Los Angeles, takes a different tack when describing the endless possibilities that lie ahead for newlyweds. She explains that the muscles and nerves that connect to help form female orgasms aren't limited to the tiny clitoris or the so-called G-spot in the upper front wall of the vagina. With exploration and patience, she says, couples can find numerous places in and around the vagina that can help bring a woman to climax. "Whether it's a G-spot exactly one-third of the way into the vagina or not, there is clitoral orgasm, there is vaginal volt orgasm, there's labial orgasm, there's mons orgasm, uterine orgasm, even rectal orgasm. I mean, there's a million ways. Everybody's a little bit different, and everybody likes something a little bit different." In other words, even if you both have orgasms during intercourse, that doesn't mean there aren't other ways to discover down the road.

One of the ways modern couples expand their repertory of sexual pleasures is by watching explicit videos. And even if couples don't feel comfortable renting them at the corner video store (especially when a seventeen-year-old clerk is working the register, holding back a smile), the world of mail order is more than willing to help: "Sensual Products: How to order them without embarrassment. How to use then without disappointment," states an ad from the Xandria Collection, a San Francisco-based vendor of what they call "sensual aids." These include such items as videos, exotic lingerie, vibrators, dildos, and Asian marital aids. (Most people don't know this company was started by the same folks who created Victoria's Secret.) The Townsend Institute and the Sinclair Institute, both of Chapel Hill, North Carolina, also offer videotaped programs by mail that tackle erotic, hard-to-discuss subjects (like clitoral stimulation and acrobatic positions of intercourse), right there on your TV, that in past generations were often never discussed by newlyweds at all.

In the name of research, I watched a copy of *Becoming Orgasmic* with a friend one night, and once we got over the embarrassment of watching a woman watching herself masturbate—with the aid of a handheld mirror and step-by-step guidebook—we agreed that it probably could help some couples who were having problems with female orgasms. It wasn't sexy, exactly, but it was more fun than reading a sex manual. I couldn't help thinking, though, about the fact that there isn't a market for sex-ed tapes for *men* on how to become orgasmic. Too easy, I guess.

What's not always easy is blending two quite different attitudes toward sex videos or pornography. Mary, thirty-two, of Seattle, feels fortunate in this regard. She told me her husband brings home *Playboy* or *Penthouse* magazines fairly regularly, and unlike some of her friends, she is not threatened or averse to them. "I like looking at them with him," she said. She also said that she gets sexually aroused by them, especially when her husband reads the letters aloud to her. "He just has to read them for five seconds and he is, well, ready," she said, not blushing a bit in her seat at the Italian restaurant at which we were dining.

Sherry Lehman, the couples counselor introduced earlier, who calls herself a "nationally acclaimed sex therapist" on the cover of her book about improving your sex life, supports the idea of watching erotic videos as a couple. But at the same time she advises using restraint and being thoughtful about the subject matter—and about *how* the subject is brought up. In other words, if X-rated tapes are sprung upon one partner and are viewed as repulsive by that partner, it might trigger major discomfort and perhaps even squelch desire. (Some psychologists suggest, during vacations early in your marriage, talking about, if not briefly trying out, the adult entertainment movies offered in hotels—but not necessarily during the honeymoon.)

Women are different when it comes to watching others, Lehman says. A woman might wonder why her husband would want to watch *other* women cavorting around naked before getting interested in and having sex with *her!* A few years ago, I spoke with Candida Royalle, a veteran New York–based video director of Femme Productions, which distributes a different kind of pornographic videos. Royalle told me she got into the business of making female-centered sex videos because there were so few videos for women to watch where *their* pleasure was foremost and up close and personal (instead of the males') right there on the screen. She played down the importance of the old standard: the hump-hump-hump nature of typical X-rated fare. Instead, she concentrated on filming—in long shots and close-ups—foreplay, manual stimulation, lots of oral sex (especially cunnilingus), and afterplay. Unfortunately, she often played down the acting skills as well. But in depicting women's orgasms more accurately than they had been shown in the past, Royalle performed a kind of public and private service to married couples across the land.

As for the future of marital aids—looking to and beyond the millennium—the computer will play a key role, erotically enhanced, of course. Already, there are signs that the Orgasmatron made famous years ago by Woody Allen in his futuristic comedy, *Sleeper,* will not seem so far-fetched by, say, 2005. Already, newlywed wives and husbands who consider themselves plugged in can walk into their local record, CD and tape, or software store and ask for a copy of *Cyborgasm.* Digi-

tally recorded, using a technique that is said to repro-
duce three-dimensional sound, the compact disc features a collection of erotic sessions—sounds, music,
moans, and sound effects—recorded in a studio using
technology that was employed for, basically, a sexier
future. "*Cyborgasm* brings to life the intimate sounds of
whispered seductions, no-holds-barred lust and mind
blowing orgasms," its promoters promise. "Listen to explicit sexual fantasies, erotic stories and voyeuristic
scenes in vivid 3-D detail." Three-D detail? Not quite, it
turns out, at least not yet.

When I asked the only married person I knew who
had heard of, bought, and listened to *Cyborgasm,* he
said it was an interesting idea and that it was almost as
titillating as a frank R-rated movie, but that "It didn't
blow me away."

Sure it sounds hokey. But who would have thought,
back around 1975, that within twenty years triple-X-
rated movies would be playing in millions of Americans'
homes nationwide, many of them rented at the corner
store or broadcast on cable television? And
many of them rented by women? Times change,
tastes change, and sexual relationships change,
which is why *Cyborgasm* may not, in the end,
be as far-fetched as it now sounds. Lisa Palac,
the producer of the risqué compact disc and
former editor of *Future Sex* magazine, simply
decided to make a novel sexual aid available to
the masses—without apology or excessive attention to community standards.

In order to have great sex throughout and
beyond the first year of your marriage, you
may find yourself at times wishing to flout
those so-called community standards.

"I treat a lot of couples where, if the guy
doesn't get sex every three days, or whatever it is, he's

"*Nobody*

crosses their own

comfort-level

boundary without

making the other

partner pay for it."

a bear," therapist Real says. "And a lot of women are afraid to say no because they're afraid they're going to lose their man." The problem that may well result is that, whether she admits it or not, Real says, a woman in this situation is going to resent her mate. And the resentment eventually will surface. "Nobody crosses their own comfort-level boundary without making the other partner pay for it," Real adds. "There's an underside to that. And it will often show up as sexual problems."

The reasoning goes like this: the same woman who can't say no is the same woman who—a year or two years later—will suddenly have headaches, vaginismus (vaginal pain preventing intercourse), or other physical ailments. In short, it is tough to have a healthy sexual relationship without both people feeling like they have control.

"If one partner is feeling controlled by the other, it's going to get screwy over time," Real says. "And unfortunately a lot of women in our culture feel they are responsible for keeping their man happy. So it's hard for them to assert their own needs."

Two—No, Three—Final Thoughts About First-Year Sex

When I asked Real, who fixes a lot of broken marriages each year at the Family Institute of Cambridge, what would be the most helpful things he could tell newlywed couples about their sexual lives, he said he would tell them two things. Then he went on to list three:

"One is, relax. Sex is not the most important part of a relationship.

"*Two* is, relax. It's not all your responsibility.

"Three is, talk to your partner about sex. Don't try and read each other's minds. Another one of those romantic ideas floating around, which is really miserable,

is that a good sexual relationship is one that nobody
needs to work on. That you just *happen* to be sexually
compatible. It's so stupid, it's so static!

"Well, you know what? Maybe you were so compatible last week, but this is *this* week. And you know,
maybe somebody's got a cold. So," he says, summing
up, "talk to each other, communicate with each other.
There's this [mistaken] notion that sex is so precious
and so romantic that it would be a step *down* from
good sex to have to talk about it. Tell each other and
show each other what you like."

You don't have to schedule a session with a sex therapist; you don't even have to utter the words "penis,"
"vagina," "clitoris," "balls," "nipples," or "anus" if you
find it uncomfortable to say them to your partner. Many
therapists explain to couples, or remind them, that
when it comes to sex and getting what you want from
your partner, communicating doesn't have to mean
speech. Many wives and husbands have already found
this out.

For instance: "There are lots of ways to communicate
during sex," Nora, thirty-four, told me, as if she were
one of Real's clients, though she's not. "You can communicate through your fingertips, for one, or your lips
or tongue. When [my husband] goes down on me, it
would help if he knew that a hard tongue hurts. The
clit hurts. I like a very slight touch. I can't tell my husband this [verbally], but I'd like to say, 'Just hold your
tongue *there*—and let me go up against you.' But if I
told him that, it would shatter him; it's such a fragile
thing to say."

"You know that old game about colder, warmer,"
Real asks, "when you put an object in the room and
say, 'You're cold,' or, 'That's warmer, warmer, warmer . . .'? There are lots of ways to let somebody know
they're doing it right. (As well as when they're not do-

ing it right.) You could just do it physically; you could moan. You let them know, 'Yeah, that's it, you got it. That's the spot.' So, yes, it doesn't have to be verbal. But it doesn't have to be nonverbal either. And a lot of it isn't just about being shy. A lot of it is this mistaken notion that if you have to talk about it, it's not great sex."

In fact, the more you do talk about it, the better the chance you'll go on to have great sex. The trick is to find a way to talk that works for you both. You might start with just a sigh.

CHAPTER 7

Newlywed

Money

SEPARATE CHECKS, JOINT ACCOUNTS, AND HARD FEELINGS

*What's yours is mine, and
what's mine is mine.*

—popular old saw, adapted from the Babylonian Talmud

I n the first few months of far too many marriages, one partner decides one day that he or she should have final say over how the money is spent. There's money trouble . . . or credit card trouble . . . and *somebody needs to take control*. Sure, you are supposed to have blended your lives together seamlessly by now, but sharing also means sharing the responsibilities. If you've gotten married you already know about two becoming one and for richer and poorer. But what about most newlywed couples, like you, who are smack in the middle, neither rich nor poor?

The toughest change you may need to make is deciding that one partner should be the money manager, even though this goes against the postfeminist conventional wisdom of everything being equal. The truth is, it isn't. Just as one partner is often the better photographer or better cook, one may be better at bill paying and keeping the debt down. Yes, the sex roles may be different from twenty-five years ago, and women run the checkbooks of many a marriage (including my own), but if the marriage is to be a true partnership, it needs to be an honest one. And sometimes that means setting pride aside.

If couples are unrealistic about money and resist this, then they may run smack into their first big fights of marriage. At the same time, it helps to know that *controlled* fights about money may not be such a terrible thing. In the long run, in fact, they may actually help a marriage, unlike nasty battles about family members, bad habits, or sex. As family therapist Arden Greenspan-Goldberg of Pomona, New York, advises, sometimes couples just need to "air it out" to clear up their insecurities about money in marriage. This is partly because money is a thing and not a person—or a feeling. It's also because money is an area of hot debate that in all likelihood they've been through before they got married, perhaps when they were planning the wedding.

"Financial problems are probably named the most in surveys about marriage, but in actuality, personality variables cause more problems than financial difficulties," William Gilbert, Ph.D., former director of the Psychological and Counseling Center at the University of Illinois at Urbana-Champaign, once told me. "If you ask a person if he would like to have more money, it's like asking if he would like to have more sex."

Over the first year of marriage, a husband and wife may have to deal with the prospect of having less of both than they thought they would have. In addition, they must also reach an understanding that dollar bills and credit cards represent much more than buying power. "They represent a struggle for raw power, too," explains Penny Bilofsky, a psychotherapist and couples counselor in the Philadelphia area.

Separate Checks, Joint Accounts, and Hard Feelings

By extension, those dollars and credit cards can also represent a loss of power. "I love to waste money, but only if it's my money," said Tine, thirty-one, a stage and set designer in New York City, who is married to Frank, thirty-five, a musician. When she put her career on hold in their first year of marriage, she lost part of her identity—her financial identity.

"In the beginning I had a big problem living on Frank's money," she said of the first few months, when things seemed to turn unequal. "Suddenly I felt I had to *justify* what I spent. Like if I bought a lipstick with Frank's money. I don't need it, maybe, but it makes me feel better."

Kathy, twenty-eight, a gift store manager from Lincoln, Nebraska, felt a different kind of money pressure as the breadwinner after her husband suddenly ended up without a job less than four months into their marriage. When it comes to paying a bill, Kathy was used to paying it immediately, whether she would take the money from her own savings account or their joint checking account. And this was not about to change, she decided, due to a change in *his* job status. "I want to be someone that other people can rely on and someone [about whom] they say, 'She pays her bills on time,' or 'She will take care of this.'" And so, she added, "I have to pay these bills and be responsible with something." He's not a flake when it comes to money, she allows; it's just that she's more organized about it. And she will firmly keep control of their funds.

Perri, thirty-three, is a Dallas-area interior designer who has designs on streamlining her and her husband's finances. "After being single and dating for five or six years after college," she said, "I was ready to start *sharing* my life, instead of just taking care of myself all the time."

"As soon as we got back from our trip after getting married," her husband Brett said, "we got a joint checking account."

"Some of my friends who are married still have separate accounts, and each pays half the bills," Perri added. "I say, 'Don't you trust each other enough to have a joint account? It seems weird to separate things—I mean, if you got married, it's supposed to be *together.*'"

On the other hand, "together" means different things to different couples. To Leslie and David (the "roller-coaster couple" in Chapter 1) being together in marriage means more to them spiritually than it does in the financial sense; perhaps because neither of them has a steady, nine-to-five job—or a predictable paycheck, for that matter. "Money is always an issue," Leslie told me, "largely because I've been freelance for years.

"We eat out almost every night," she added. "And we split the bill. The other night someone we were out with saw this and said: 'You guys are *still* doing that? *Splitting* the bill?' I know people come up with these fancy complicated accounts, but we're just not ready for that yet. We opened *one* joint account, so we'd have a place to put the checks we got for wedding gifts, but we basically do it fifty-fifty.

"Did you see *The Joy Luck Club?*" Leslie asked, referring to the 1993 film based on the novel of the same name by Amy Tan. "There's a scene where a couple splits *everything* . . . to the penny. He decides he shouldn't have to pay for her tampons, and she decides she shouldn't have to pay for his ice cream that she doesn't eat.

"In our marriage, we don't really shop for food. That's part of the problem; we go out all the time. But if I'm going to get some coffee or something, I'll say, 'Dave, give me a twenty'; then I put in a twenty [into the kitty]. I'm the anal one, the organized one. It goes in my wallet."

At which point in our talk she handed her wallet over for inspection. It looked like a fairly normal leather wallet and change purse combo, except for one thing: there was a wad of green bills in the change purse portion, stuffed with nickels, dimes and quarters, and then, behind the Blockbuster Video "Rent Six Get One Free" rental card, there was a separate stash of cash. It turns out this was her and David's common cash, their pooled, weekend, household-shopping kitty. You know, for the necessities, which include a video rental or two once in a while when they need a break from their work.

"Or," Leslie said, "I might buy a new dress and then put it in the back of the closet—without telling Dave. Then I'll work it slowly toward the front . . . after a few weeks. Then I'll put it on, and he might say, 'Is that a new dress?' And I'll say, '*This* old thing?' It's that kind of thinking. And I'm guilty of it."

Yours, Mine, and Whose?

This notion of yours, mine, and ours is the major sociological difference in money management among newly wedded couples over the past twenty years. It might have seemed frighteningly defensive in the 1950s, 1960s, and early 1970s, but it is almost expected among newlyweds of the mid-1990s, at least for some part of the first year. Partly this is due to couples getting married later, on average, than they did in prior generations: many partners in this generation have established a financial identity before getting married. Used to be, you didn't do that until you got married. For many, *marrying* was a way to get established financially. Not in this era, though, of variable-rate credit card offers in the mail, ATMs, gold cards galore, and college-loan debt that typically sticks with a couple for five to ten years. . . .

Anna, thirty, of San Diego, California, married Jared, thirty-four, a photographer and sole proprietor, in 1993, and quickly got the picture. "I quit my job two months into our marriage to help him out with his business," she said, "and right away it felt weird. "

Why?

Because, she said, she felt as if she *had* given up a part of her identity.

"I was scared to death," she said. "You see, I [only] have signing authority of Jared's business account. He's the sole owner of it, even though I have signing privileges and, if something were to happen to us, legally it's half mine. It's just that I'm not on the paperwork. But I was afraid to death at first to write checks for me out of his account. I still have a hard time taking money out of his account."

At first, it didn't matter whether it was for business expenses like film processing or for household ones like groceries. It's just hard for Anna to do. "We have two accounts," she explained. "We have my old checking account that I use to go to the grocery store and stuff, and I make him give me an allowance every month so I don't have to ask him for money or I don't have to write checks out of his business account."

Although both Anna's and Jared's names are on the account she draws her allowance from, it's clear that they both still refer to it as hers. Because it's the one she feels more comfortable with. At the same time, she actually prefers to have her husband write her a check each month for these expenses; it may seem weird to some couples, but it feels right to them.

"He said, 'Well, just write yourself checks whenever you want,' but I said no, '*You* write me a check.'" In her own way, Anna likes to think she's earned the household spending money and her personal spending cash by working for her husband's business. That's why she wouldn't feel as comfortable if she were just to cash checks whenever she felt the impulse.

"I mean, I have access to his money and he has access to mine," she explained, "even though it's still separate. But all of our bills and everything are paid out of his business account, and at first I was afraid to death to pay my car payment or my house payment out of it. Now [ten months into the marriage], I'm getting a little more used to it."

Anna has become the de facto chief financial officer of the marriage. And so far it's working just fine, even though her husband owns the business. This has happened, it turns out, for good reason, since she said she has always been more responsible about paying bills.

"Before we got married," Anna said, "he was always delinquent on everything. I have a schedule—a book—that I write all the checks in, and it lists what check number, when I paid it, who I paid it to, how much the balance is. Used to be, he just paid whatever whenever he got around to it." She paused. And conceded: "No organizational skills at all on his part."

Which sounds quaint, almost, in an informal interview, but could actually spell trouble in the future. As Craig Aronoff, head of the Family Enterprise Center at Kennesaw State College in Marietta, Georgia, has said, "A new business is a risky venture and marriage can be precarious enough. You risk an awful lot when you combine the two."[1]

Jared and Anna also have one other area of merged money, a stash of cash on hand that they keep, one that is not unlike Leslie and David's pooled fund mentioned earlier. "We usually have about four hundred dollars cash," Anna said, "for either one of us just to grab and use. It's in a drawer. The *money drawer*. I know it sounds weird. But it works."

Prenuptial Pronouncements

Terrence Netzky, fifty-two, is a Chicago-based attorney who specializes in estate planning and whose clients tend to be big hitters (including a professional athlete or two), millionaires, corporate magnates, and other society-page notables. On a recent Thursday morning, he walked briskly into the city's plush East Bank Health Club and flashed his membership card. He climbed the stairs and headed straight to the club's café: it was time for business, which today meant the money business of marriage. As in, Which partner brought what to the household? and, How should they take account of that?

"Most people don't understand," he says, "that a prenuptial agreement is more necessary than ever before because today the minute you say, 'I do,' you already did!" However, the news in new marriages is that if you were careless enough in this regard to have married without a prenup, as they say, all is not lost. In fact, Netzky says, in some cases (in some states) you can rectify the oversight with a *postnuptial* agreement signed afterward.

For it turns out that in all states there are fixed rights that accrue to each spouse along with the marriage. No matter how much in love you may feel three months before the wedding, these rights are worth knowing about. Just in case . . . For starters, fixed rights are divided between death rights and divorce rights. With *death rights,* Netzky says, "if you don't have a premarital agreement, when you say, 'I do,' you just gave your spouse something. In many states, it's one half of everything you own if you don't have children [or one third if you do]." It's different with *divorce rights,* though. These don't include (in most states) the property that was acquired prior to the marriage or anything obtained afterward by inheritance or as a gift. "This is generally nonmarital or separate property," Netzky says. It may be wise, then, for you to check with your family's lawyer about your state's divorce or death rights.

He cites as an example one of the legendary premarital death rights cases that took place in the Midwest some years ago, involving a multimillionaire philanthropist. The ink was barely dry on his and his bride's prenuptial agreement when the aging groom walked his third wife to the altar, escorted her to their wedding reception, and then fell into a coma from which he never awakened. The new "Mrs. Philanthropist" was entitled to whatever they had agreed to in the prenuptial contract—even though she'd only been married a few hours and, in the view of some, hadn't actually earned it.

On the other end of the scale were Leslie and Mike, who are a happily married Dallas-area couple today, but who started out with a lot more love than they had money. If they had gotten overly stressed by money problems, they might not have survived more than six months into their marriage. But they didn't, and at the time of our meeting they were about to celebrate their first anniversary. And as Leslie, twenty-eight, tells it, the worst of it wasn't so bad after all. You see, before landing in the Southwest, they moved to San Diego "on a whim and said, 'We'll get jobs, we have enough money for two months.'" They thought wrong. Things cost more in California than they had planned, so their community property was minimal, to say the least.

"We had an apartment; we had a cooler that was our table," Leslie told me almost proudly. "We had those 'egg crate' pads that we put on the carpet and used as mattresses; we had a Swiss army knife—our only knife. And I can honestly say it was the best time in our lives."

At this, her husband, Mike, smiled and piped in, "We also had a Sony TV square that—to watch it at night—I would lay on my stomach and prop it up, and we would both watch it. That was it. We had no furniture, no cleaning supplies, we had nothing. It was great."

"If we had to go back to that, *damn,* it wouldn't be tough," said Leslie, who now has a job at The Limited clothing store.

Except that by now, well into their first year of marriage, their views have changed as their bank accounts and expectations have grown. And as a symbol, perhaps, of this growth, their major mode of transportation has changed from a little old Toyota to a big new Isuzu Trooper. At three months into the marriage, Mike noticed a distinct change in his spending and saving habits and a newfound maturity that surprised him. As a result, he began to view himself differently, as much more responsible.

In a way Mike believes his wife has a right to freedom from financial worry, if not exactly financial freedom. "I just feel like I have to show my wife respect, I have to learn respect, and when the time comes I have to show her that she can rely on me in difficult situations." Fortunately, it seems, their most difficult situations concerning money and early marriage are behind them, as Leslie is working and Mike gets ready to finish business school and pursue some kind of job in marketing.

His and Her Property Rights

The irony in all this worry and finagling over finance in modern marriages is not lost on social scientists who study marriage as a custom. When asked for advice about money and marriage, they remind newly wedded couples that the institution of marriage—in fact the whole idea of it—was born out of economic need and agreement. The rite of marriage, the bond of marriage, among earlier civilizations was little more than a ceremonial prenup: the husband and wife came together in fixed marriage to keep the family wealth in good standing as well as in the family. Sounds heartless today, but it was the rule in the days of knights on white horses.

But that was then. Today, in 57 percent of all marriages, the wife works. And in those households, there's a good chance she worked before the wedding. Not only did she enter the relationship as an equal partner, but she also very likely was a financial equal, or even the primary wage earner. Add this to the fact that many couples move after marriage, "to start a new life," and that one or the other partner quits or can't find a job, and there is potential for conflict right away—a sense of uncompensated loss.

When the loss escalates, or a partner gets into a pattern of money squabbles or uses money in excessive, distorted, or destructive ways, says Susan Forward, an author and a former therapist of Nicole Brown Simpson, this person is being driven by what she calls "money demons."[2] That may be overstating the case a bit (Forward also wrote the book *Toxic Parents*), but she makes a good point. Money is not the whole problem—it's what's behind the irresponsible use of it in a relationship that matters.

If money differences, pressures of job change, or moving happen to cause a couple to separate, they should know that divorce laws in the United States differ greatly in different states. Borders count, and they may count for a lot. Several Midwestern states and most Western states, such as Texas, California, Idaho, and Washington, still follow laws modeled after Spanish civil law, which distinguishes between community (marital) and separate (nonmarital) property. *Marital property* is property that is earned and received together at the wedding and thereafter. *Nonmarital property* is inherited property or gifts that are received individually and unrelated to the marriage. Furthermore, nothing received, bought, or earned before the wedding is typically considered community, or marital, property in these states.

Netzky suggests, "The laws of the state in which you're living at the time of the divorce will usually govern your divorce—which is why some people will pick up and establish residency in a 'more friendly' state before they get a divorce." But most states also will recognize the laws of the state in which the marriage took place and where the couple was living, if they had a prenuptial agreement in that state.

"It's a fact that this generation needs prenuptial agreements more than any other generation in history," Netzky says. "One reason is that they've earned more money earlier than generations before." A second reason is that, on average, they've accumulated money, assets, and investments separately, and well before the wedding. Also, many elderly middle-class parents are giving the Baby Boomers more gifts today and are leaving more inheritance than previous generations did. Add the fact that more of the Baby Boomers' marriages are likely to be shorter than their parents', and many of them will have more marriages than earlier genera-

Baby

Boomers' marriages

are likely to be shorter.

tions. And so, because there is quite often an assumption that marriage may well end in divorce, perhaps soon, it's a good idea to have some pre-arranged agreements about who gets what from whom.

However, some newlyweds or soon-to-be-marrieds *are* clever enough to turn these marriages and their related prenuptial agreements into assets. Take Liza, a striking-looking flight attendant, who in her early twenties met a wealthy stock market analyst who was in his fifties and was worth between $60 and $70 million. They had been married a year when she divorced him and received the $1 million stipulated in their prenuptial agreement. (*Then* he sold his ranch for $60 million.)

It didn't take long for Liza to find another wealthy Wall Street type, this one in his forties, and she figured the same thing would happen again. Unfortunately, this fellow didn't want any prenuptial agreement, since he was willing to take his chances, and Liza was foolish enough to agree. She just assumed he would continue to earn more than she did. She was wrong. He had a bad year. Her interest on the million dollars she had invested was more than he earned—and at the end of that year, when they divorced in Illinois, they had to divide community income they earned in *half,* and he came out the winner.

Netzky, who estimates he's executed over one hundred prenuptial agreements in his twenty-six years of practice, occasionally has been hired by parents to break an engagement. "One wealthy couple came to me because their son, who was an officer in the family business and their heir apparent, was engaged to a woman they found undesirable," he recalls. "My clients felt the daughter-in-law's personality was so dictatorial she would be running the business if, God forbid, something happened to the son. So they asked me to write a prenuptial agreement so ironclad it would make her break the engagement. I did, and it did."

The contract called for the bride to give up all rights she could ever have in anything the man inherited, including the business, the business appreciation, or earnings. They were extremely stringent provisions. The minute her attorney read it he called Netzky and said there was no way he'd let the bride-to-be sign it, and he started to negotiate, stating things he felt she should be entitled to. "You don't understand. This is not negotiable," Netzky told him, sounding like a television law-show legal whiz. That was on a Thursday. Saturday morning the marriage was called off. "She kept the three-carat diamond, and to this day the parents still thank me, and it was several years ago," Netzky recalls.

Sometimes a prenuptial agreement can act as the glue to keep a marriage together, as was the case with one other couple Netzky worked with. "He was a double-digit zillionaire in his sixties," Netzky said, "and she was in her forties. He asked me to set up a very specific agreement with very clear goals: if the marriage lasted one year, she would get X amount of dollars; if it lasted two years, she got Y amount; and so on in increments that got larger each year the marriage lasted."

Unfortunately, there were no clauses about happiness in the marriage. For it turned out this woman made her husband miserable. Still, she has stuck it out because she wants more money . . . in the end. Whenever he sees her, she refers to Netzky as "that bastard who did our prenuptial agreement and screwed me." "But so far," Netzky says, "it's kept the marriage together."

If you or your partner are concerned about these issues, contact the American Academy of Matrimonial

Lawyers in Chicago, (312) 263-6477; or the Academy of Family Mediators in Golden Valley, Minnesota, (612) 525-8670.

Postnuptial Agreements Have Arrived

Occasionally attorneys have been asked to write a postnuptial agreement (or modify a prenuptial) immediately after a marriage, when a couple has eloped or married impetuously, and one or both parties—or families—are worried. What's this mean? Well, the "impetuous" part means on impulse, not reason. But as for the "postnup" part, it means sooner is better than later, but later is better than never. Most people don't even know there's such a thing as a postnuptial agreement. They assume it's too late to consider such a thing once they've said their vows. (Again, it depends on the state in which you live.) It makes sense for many couples, though, to write and sign a postnuptial agreement shortly after they return from their honeymoon. After all, that's often when they set about combining bank accounts, drafting wills, talking with their lawyer(s), and/or buying new kinds of insurance, as a couple. Plus, it won't spoil the romance of the last few weeks leading up to the wedding day.

It turns out, moreover, there's often no legal time limit for crafting and signing such agreements. When they are drawn up and written, though, they generally are completed within a few months of the ceremony. One such case involved a Chicago couple in their late twenties who ran off to Las Vegas to get married one weekend without telling their parents. The bride, whose family had millions, ran into trouble when she got back.

"Her grandmother told her she would be taken out

of the will if she didn't get a postnuptial agreement the next day," says Netzky. "So I wrote it, they both signed it, and I called the grandmother and reported it had been executed, and she was relieved. Of course, they might have ripped it up once they got outside my door. I'll never know. But for their sake I hope they didn't."

There's one more problem that can be avoided in a separation soon after marriage—if the couple has been wise about separating gifts. Anything given to them immediately after the wedding becomes community, or marital, property in most states, which means it's to be divided equitably if they divorce soon, no matter which side it came from, *unless* there's a prenuptial agreement. If one or the other received personal gifts or checks before the ceremony that were made out to him or her personally, it is ordinarily not community property.

"But if the check was made out to both partners, or it was made out to one and he or she is careless enough to place it into a joint account with no prenuptial agreement—it goes right back into that 'land of fifty–fifty' that minute they say, 'I do,'" Netzky warns.

Remember: in many states, by the time you say, "I do," you already did.

A FINANCIAL GOALS WORKSHEET

For each of the following financial goals, identify its importance to you (high, medium, low, none), and indicate whether achieving the objective is a Short-term goal (S), Medium-term (M), or Long-term (L). Compare your answers; you may need to rethink some plans.

OBJECTIVE	TERM	IMPORTANCE HIGH	MEDIUM	LOW
SPENDING & LIFESTYLE				
Improve Present Standard of Living (spending)	____	____	____	____
Financial Independence at Age ___	____	____	____	____
New Home	____	____	____	____
New Car/Truck/ Extensive Travel	____	____	____	____
DEPENDENT SUPPORT				
Own Education (college, graduate school,)	____	____	____	____
Children's Education	____	____	____	____
Support Siblings/ Elderly Parents	____	____	____	____
SAVING & INVESTMENT				
Build Financial Cushion	____	____	____	____
Build Retirement Fund	____	____	____	____
Start or Change Career	____	____	____	____

Source: *First Comes Love, Then Comes Money*, (Currency/ Doubleday); interview with Susan Maxwell, marriage and family therapist, Beverly Hills, California.

CHAPTER 8

"What Are We Fighting For?"

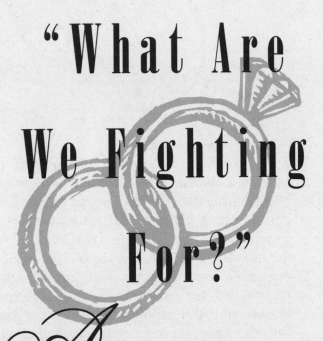

A good way of getting another person focused
upon you is, of course, to engage that person
in a fight.

—Maggie Scarf, *Intimate Partners*

*N*ot everyone likes surprises, but they are inevitable in the first year of marriage. What you get from the one you love isn't necessarily what you *thought* you'd get, and a surprise may be followed by friction or anger. For instance, when a Minneapolis couple, Rosemary and Jeff, were dating, Rosemary used to get a kick out of telling her friends that her boyfriend—a thirty-five-year-old—bought and read action-adventure comic books for fun. One, two, maybe three a week. But after they got married, it wasn't so fun for Rosemary when Jeff would read a stack of them on the living room couch on a sunny weekend day while she wanted to go outside and run or ride bikes together. She was angry at him and let him know. HOW could he prefer to spend his weekends like THAT? she wondered. This was not whom she married. Or was it? Something would have to change. . . . It did. He now reads his *Captain Americas* in the bathroom, to where they've been banished, and if you want to know the truth, he probably takes a little longer in there these days than he needs to.

This kind of early marital annoyance that builds to frustration can be avoided or eased in a number of ways, one of which couples counselors call, rather stuffily, "renegotiating your personal marriage contract." And odd as it may sound at first, this rethinking can work wonders. Oftentimes couples can do the negotiating by themselves. Other times they may need the help of a therapist to guide them along.

Phyllis Levy is one such guide. As a licensed and certified social worker, she also serves as director of the All About Women Counseling Center in Arlington Heights, Illinois. Having seen hundreds of newlyweds trudge through her doors, she believes people in general tend to look at marriage in a fairly static way. Unfortunately most marriages aren't static or fixed; they change profoundly from Day One through Year Fifty, and especially in the first 365 days.

Learning How to Fight

Midway through their first year, Sandy, twenty-nine, and Kris, thirty-seven, of Phoenix, Arizona, were beginning to think it was all over. Sandy had their first baby just six months into their marriage—way earlier than they had planned—and Kris, a graphic designer, had been married once before and had a son of his own. There were complexities from the get-go.

"When I went to the doctor and found out I was pregnant," Sandy said, "I called him [Kris] right away. I knew what I was going to do; I was going to have the baby. And he said, 'Well, let's get married.' And I was shocked." They got married soon after, and Sandy began to notice that through her entire pregnancy, "He was totally there for me, being nice, nice, nice, nice, nice. And I was so *mean!*" In short, she said, she was "young and unprepared" when his son came to live with them just two weeks after they got married. "And so I'm thinking: I'm married to a guy who has an ex-wife. Plus, he's a perfectionist. It was a lot."

When Sandy and Kris first got married, she continued, "he was too dominant for me; I couldn't handle it. He had to be right all the time and he *was* right ninety-nine percent of the time. (And I couldn't stand that.)" She didn't know what she needed him to do exactly, but she knew Kris would need to change his behavior toward her if they were going to survive as a couple.

Kris also knew that he was committed to this marriage. He knew that for them, at least, the first few years might be the hardest. And they were. But the two of them also found strength in three things: their family, church, and therapy. Each of these institutions helped them negotiate the profound changes in their emotions and family makeup.

"Kids just make you want to try harder," Sandy said. "What happened was, we thought we wanted to get a divorce, and I was scared to death—I didn't want to get one. I was getting used to so many things, and learning how to fight, and learning what's fair and what's not, and that you can't play dirty."

She learned a lot of that in therapy—in their second year of marriage.

"I was insecure," she said. But what came out in the counseling, she added, was that when they would get into fights, she would "freak out. I would fight every fight like I was losing him. But once we found out that I needed to know we were going to *stay married no matter what,* this [freak-out] fighting never really happened again."

For his part, Kris had already been through the frenzied ups and downs of a previous marriage and divorce, complicated by the child he and his ex-wife had

had together. He had become part of a benumbing modern-day demographic: that more than 1.3 million couples get divorced each year across the United States. Early in his marriage to Sandy, he drew upon a willingness to work on issues (and on his career) that he built upon over time—and that he hadn't been able to forge in his first marriage.

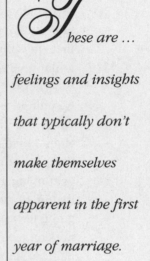

These are ... feelings and insights that typically don't make themselves apparent in the first year of marriage.

"Kris needs to know, as hard as he works, that someone thinks he is really *'bad,'* " Sandy said jokingly. "You know, such a stud! And to me he is. I mean, I don't treat him like he's king all the time! But I know when he needs it—I know when he's at the end of his rope and he's tired of me and the kids just from normal, monotonous shit. I know when you need to take time and just clear stuff out. I know when it's time to treat him like a king. And he tells me I'm beautiful, and that he loves me, all the time."

These are the kinds of feelings and insights that typically don't make themselves apparent in the first year of marriage, although the problems sometimes do. It's taken Sandy and Kris more than six years to get where they are today, and it just happened that the first one and a half were the toughest.

So when the marriage changes, it's good to know how to go about changing the foundation—the contract—for the better. "It is often [incorrectly] fixed in an 'If you really loved me, you'd do this' tap dance," Phyllis Levy says. "But not only is it fixed in that way; most couples also believe that contracts are going to be magically negotiated simply from love and caring feelings."

Surprise! The problem is, that kind of thinking doesn't

take into account what happens when *my* needs conflict drastically with *your* needs. Fresh from the altar,
like Kris and Sandy, most couples don't yet have the
skills for renegotiating these needs. Nor do they have
society's permission to do that. Society tends to reserve
that for the longtime marrieds. While the general view
of hanging around is that things are just supposed to
work out, most couples don't want to concede early on
that they often don't. And they may not want to talk
about it, either.

"Where did we ever get the idea that there is to be
no pain in a good relationship?" writes therapist Cranor
Graves in his straightforward guide *Building a Marriage.* "In marriage, the choice is between the construc-
tive pain of dealing with conflict or the destructive pain
of running away from it."[1] Graves goes further and says
that in a way, it's like going to the dentist. You know it's
going to be painful, but if you have a cavity or a filling
missing, you show up in the office ready to trade some
pain for future comfort.

Colleen, 32, of Albuquerque, remembers the pain
she felt in her first year of marriage—pain that followed
a bad habit her husband, Eddie, had of keeping certain
things secret from her. He wouldn't lie, exactly; he
would simply refrain from telling her when his old girlfriend would call him. This would happen every six
weeks or so at first, and he would only admit that
she called when Colleen would confront him: "Has
Joan called lately?" she'd ask. "Yeah," he'd answer, feeling guilty.

This would set her off and they would fight big-time,
because Colleen felt betrayed by *both* Joan-the-wench
and Eddie. Why, she wondered, couldn't he tell her
when these calls came? Was he trying to hide something? If so, what?? "No, I'm not hiding anything," he'd
say to Colleen. "I just don't tell you because you get all

upset. And it doesn't mean anything anyway." Obviously it did mean something, or she wouldn't have gotten so angry. And he had to learn that this ex-girl*friend* might have been playing tricks. The upshot? Joan doesn't call anymore.

"It's difficult to say, 'We have a contract that says this and this, but it isn't working for me, so I want to renegotiate it,'" Phyllis Levy says. "That's pretty scary." She's right, and it's partly scary because it sounds so, well, *cold:* "contracts," "negotiation," "working." These aren't the words that trip off the tongue when you think of newlyweds in love. It also implies that "We're not as perfect together" as we'd want everyone to think we are. So, Levy explains, too many couples stick their heads in the sand and keep working at the "If you really love me, you'd do that tap dance."

How, then, do you negotiate a new contract? A first step is to ask yourselves: what is the essence of what you want to get, here and now and into the future? Most couples don't need to go to a professional counselor for that. It depends upon what kind of skills people have and how articulate they are. It also depends on how accessible a couple's own needs and wishes are and how able they are to speak up when they're disappointed and angry.

Are You a Conflict Avoider?

Disappointment, it almost goes without saying, doesn't set in overnight. In many cases newlyweds become adept at avoiding conflict. They may be unhappy because they fear that renegotiating the terms of their marriage will mean conflict and criticism. They know that, if you take the risk, there will be a rocky time as you're banging out the new contract, because admitting

you're not 100 percent perfect is a tough admission.
Men are trained to "sort of do what the situation calls
for," Levy says. If they're playing on a football team
and the quarterback says "take this position," the guy
doesn't start arguing about the sense of the directive,
he just does it because he wants to be a team player.
And it's the same at work. Men are not taught to go in
to the boss and put the job on line and say, 'Look, this
isn't really working for me.'

"They do what the team asks, and also, they're
scared they'll lose their jobs," Levy adds. "That happens
in marriages too. They don't want to rock any boats. So
men become good numb-ers—they *numb* themselves;
they *get through* things."

One way to end this numbing is mentioned prominently in *We Can Work it Out* by Howard Markman,
Ph.D., and Clifford Notarius, Ph.D., a book that was
highly touted at the fifty-first annual convention of marriage and family therapists held in Anaheim, California.
Basically, the authors say, you've got to cut the biting
"zingers" when you fight, but you also have to learn
that conflict can be okay.

Personally, I found some of the Markman/Notarius
advice truly useful in my own first year of marriage—
the chapter called "Hot Thoughts: The Fuel of Destructive Relationship Conflicts." The authors advised
couples to avoid "Always-Never self talk." Sounds easy
enough; I'm always reading advice like that. But seriously, they point out that saying "never" and "always"
in fights tend to heighten the character-assassination
feelings that are bound to come up anyway, at least
occasionally. They can lead, Notarius and Markman
say, to feelings of hopelessness and despair. And more
important, they can prevent couples from recognizing
the exceptions to these charges—these "always's" and

"never's"—that might otherwise become the basis for positive change.[2]

"I'm very aware that you're not supposed to do that," my wife, Paula, told me, when I informed her of these fighting rules two months into our marriage. "So when I say it, I hear it. And I have to stop myself, because I say, 'You *always* work . . . ,' or, 'You *never* stop and think how I feel.' And when I say it, I know it's not true. As soon as I say it I go, 'Agggghh!'"

We were guilty as charged, except . . . "*You're* the one who says I don't fight fair. But you're not a fighter at all," Paula said—provoking me *almost* into an argument. "I'm not sure you're in it with me until I get a reaction! That's one reason why I do it." Forget for a moment the always-never talk. By not fighting at all, I wasn't fighting fairly.

The issues of renegotiation usually center around who has the power and control over what in the marriage, and they can get played out in any number of ways, such as in how we spend our leisure time: do we spend it with my family or yours, our friends or yours? When the wedding pictures come back and the wedding dress is packed away, you start weighing the standard of living you both expect and what kind of housekeeping is going to be necessary. Who's going to do that housework? And if I disagree with your standard of living, am I responsible for doing the extra work to keep it that high? Who has what job? And when it gets right down to it, who has the real say about what becomes really important?

"Fortunately, things are changing, but even now many women typically have had a hard time expressing their dissatisfaction with the way things are going, because they don't want to admit their marriage isn't perfect," Phyllis Levy explains. "Because that would imply some kind of failure on their part. And many men don't seem to even know when they're dissatisfied because most of them are not as in touch with their feelings as women are, and they're not as sharply attuned to what's going on for them."

That's what happened between Laura and Ken, a Chicago couple who weren't able to confront and work out these problems: their marriage ended after only six months. Laura, an artist, was twenty-four when she met Ken, a successful twenty-six-year-old freelance photographer, who soon became the love—and very center—of her life. Although they immediately decided to see no one else, they didn't move in together until after their mega-wedding. "No ring, no fling," Laura was fond of saying with a laugh. A former cheerleader and homecoming queen with the proverbial soft blond hair and big blue eyes, Laura excitedly planned the "wedding of the year." And although she came from a simple home, no expense was spared, because Ken, a small, quiet, slightly built man, came from a society family that would foot all the bills. In fact, Laura was swept into a world of private clubs and designer labels that no doubt dazzled her. "But I couldn't have loved him more if he'd been impoverished," she said. He was also romantic and caring, creative in his courtship, and dearly loving in his obvious admiration of everything about her.

An Unlikely Arrangement

"He acted as though I was a gift from heaven; he couldn't believe how wonderful I was, and I felt we were the perfect couple and certainly destined to have the perfect marriage," Laura said. There were no warnings, no red flags, but on the honeymoon she began to feel uncomfortable with him. "I just felt that something

was going on that wasn't quite right. But I couldn't figure out what it was, so I dismissed it," she said. It took
only a few months for her to realize she had made
some kind of terrible mistake; that Ken was obsessed
with jealousy and a need to control her life that within
six months absolutely destroyed her self-esteem.

"He had bought a house before our wedding and
didn't tell me about it until after the deal had closed,"
Laura recalled. "I didn't think of that as a warning, but
now, looking back, I realize that he never asked my
opinion. It was in a terrible neighborhood that I didn't
want to live in, and he just assumed I'd go along with
whatever he decided. And I did." She had also begun
furnishing her own apartment with an eye toward how
those furnishings would fit into his home when they
eventually married.

"When we unpacked my things after the honeymoon
and I put out my beautiful bedroom set with the com-
forter, curtains, and dust ruffle and pillows that I sewed
myself, he looked at them with contempt and said, 'I
didn't know Laura Ashley was moving in with us!' At the
time I laughed and thought that was a pretty clever re-
mark." It was also wickedly mean. "The next night he
made me go out shopping with him, and we bought a
stark modern bed and decorated the bedroom in mini-
malist modern spread and window shades—and all my
things were moved into the guest room. But I still didn't
get it."

A few weeks later, Laura decided to throw her first
big party, in honor of Ken's birthday—and in so doing
she was to invite both of their families and friends to
see their new home. She started working on the party
every night after she got home from the office and all
through weekends, cooking and freezing gourmet
foods, cleaning the house and polishing all the new silver, and setting out the best china. And she loved doing

it all. But there were three big boxes in the hall that hadn't yet been unpacked, and Laura couldn't move them herself. So she kept asking and asking Ken to help her do it.

"Suddenly he turned on me, and I stopped in my tracks, because that was the first moment of truth," Laura remembered. "He said, 'If I were having a party for you, you'd have a fit if I asked you to help me!' And I realized he wasn't going to help, and it scared me. I had a flashback to the way my dad used to talk to my mother when I was very little, before he left her for a much younger woman, and I was suddenly afraid I'd gotten myself into the same kind of deal. But it took my mom twenty years to get out, because she'd gone from my grandfather's house to my father's and never worked a day in her life. She was afraid to rock the boat with two little kids." In other words, that was the deal she had negotiated by default.

Laura, meanwhile, was so frightened by the exchange that she decided then and there to *change*. She decided she would do anything she could to make her new husband more pleasant. "I was willing to adapt, but all of a sudden nothing I did was right." When she worked late, which was often, her husband accused her of just sitting at her desk after 5 P.M. so she wouldn't have to come home and be with him.

Trying mightily to adapt, she also made a habit of shopping and preparing gourmet meals on the weekends, then freezing them so that Ken could eat homemade lunches and dinners every day. But then he complained that she spent all her time in the kitchen instead of sitting with him and watching television. He accused her of spending too much time talking on the phone to her mother; he didn't like the way she kept writing to her younger brother in college and sending care packages to him. Jealousy—or sickness? He thought she saw her girlfriends too often, and he timed her when she went to the grocery store.

"It got crazy," Laura said. Clearly, the situation was beyond the scope of the self-help books. "So one day only three months after the wedding, I asked him if we could sit down on the couch and try to work out our problems," she said. "I told him I wanted to talk about why I wasn't happy even though I was trying to do everything he asked me to. He said he had assumed that we were happy. In fact, he was astonished that I had anything to complain about. He assumed that since I now had a lot more money and could buy just about anything I wanted for the first time in my life, that would have made me very happy. And although that was a thrill, and our furnishings and wedding gifts did provide a more beautiful home than I'd ever lived in, it didn't make for happiness."

He had assumed that we were happy.

Six months after the wedding, after Laura started to really dislike herself, she arranged for herself and Ken to get professional counseling. And as soon as they began doing the little exercises their therapist gave them, Laura realized they could never work things out. "One of the exercises was to each write a list of eight things we didn't like about the other," she recalled. "And on his list he wrote that I was too generous, too nice to my family, too involved with my friends, too conscientious about my job, too thoughtful about giving gifts, spent too much time cooking and cleaning. After I took one look at that list I decided that I was a pretty good person. It also made me realize he was like a child, desperate to say something bad but not really having anything to complain about."

Laura began to have headaches and anxiety attacks, and one night she woke up out of a nightmare and said to herself, "I'm getting out of here. I've stayed too long."

There was no contract worth even trying to renegotiate. It wasn't easy to leave so soon after that elaborate wedding, but she went out and found a studio apartment near her office, rented it, then went back home, took a deep breath, and told Ken she was going to leave. "I was scared, but I didn't care. I was out of there!" she recalled. "Now I think that although he was a wonderful fiancé, the moment we said, 'I do,' he saw me as property, the way he completely owned his perfect home and cameras and all. We were in a battle for control over *me*."

"I've aged a lot since then and I'm only twenty-eight," Laura said. "I don't take crap as easily, and I don't let people say things to me that upset me without telling them anymore. This month is exactly one year since our wedding, but I'm coming out of the awful depression that started when I lost my self-esteem. When I moved into my place, I was so alone, and I was foolishly concerned about how people were reacting. After all, it was very embarrassing to have planned and talked about a wedding for a whole year and then walk out on it so fast." Now that it's over, she realizes that certain mean-spirited people may have gossiped for a few minutes about her in the hallways at work, but when they went out to lunch they soon forgot about Laura and her problems.

"The main thing was," Laura said, "that I realize I didn't deserve to be treated that way and I didn't allow it to go on." Taking a cue, perhaps, from authors Markman and Notarius, Laura also realized there has to be something to work *on* before you can fight the good fight to "work it out." "It would have been nice if we could have gotten back to the wonderful relationship we had before the wedding," she said, "but that takes two grown-ups. We only had one—and that was me."

Are You Your Job? Is He? Is She?

More often today, rather than a spouse's personality changing markedly after the wedding, a job or job situation changes. Which means the way you view your spouse or yourself—or both—may change in ways you can't easily prepare for.

In an instructive article in *Psychology Today* not long ago, family therapists Barry Dym and Michael Glenn sketched out a "Forecast for Couples"—in regard to job and other conflicts—by analyzing what it is that sets married couples apart. One of the observations they made was that quite often today, ten "hallmark" words of complaint are heard in counseling sessions, no matter how much people think they have learned lately about love and relationships: "This is not the person I thought I had married." Or they may offer a slightly different, fifteen-word version: "If I had known then what I know today, I never would have married her [or him]."[3]

Their conclusion: people may simply expect too much from each other nowadays, and for good reason. Expectations about marriage have changed. We expect our partners to be passionate lovers and also loyal confidantes. We want them to bond with us intensely at times, but we also want and *need* them to give us our space. These demands are different from those of two generations ago; new permutations for possible conflicts have arisen. Similarly, we want romance in the quiet times of marriage, but we also want a stable partner to nurture the kids, run the household, and share the stresses of the family's career concerns, whether it be a one- or two-income household.

The married couple is supposed to be "a stable haven in a cool, hostile, unpredictable world," Dym and Glenn write, even though today, in too many households, the stability is elusive and surprises too often arise.

"I think marriages should be negotiated as often as we negotiate business contracts," says Phyllis Levy just a bit cynically. "If marriages were treated like businesses, we'd be in much better shape. Every year you'd have an evaluation of your performance: it would include a performance review and budget reviews, and you'd both ask, 'Is this working for you and for me, and is it profitable for both? And am I getting what I need and want, and are you?' That's a general formula that most people can use."

Erin and Kevin, a newly wedded Chicago couple in their twenties, knew each other in high school, became serious while in college, and continued to date monogamously while they were starting their careers. Over a series of conversations and a couple of Christmases, things evolved to an understanding that one day when they both felt comfortable with the idea, they would marry and start a family.

Erin got settled first: she quickly got a job in a large communications corporation and rose to a top manager's position within a year. She was secure, well liked, destined for even more promotions, and, most important, had a good annual income with excellent benefits. Kevin, on the other hand, viewed that time after college as his only opportunity to live as a free spirit, and took a very low paying job working for a nonprofit organization overseas for two years.

Although they were separated, the pair wrote letters and postcards and talked regularly by phone and had marvelously romantic vacations together all over Europe. When he returned to the States and they moved into an apartment together, Kevin made a couple of attempts at nine-to-five jobs but was discontented ("bummed," was actually how he put it) because he found the jobs so boring. Plus, he couldn't cope with corporate life after the freedom of his European experience. Finally, when both of them were twenty-seven, and although Kevin's career was still unsettled, he gave Erin an engagement ring, and they began to make their long-awaited wedding plans.

"At the time, since I had a very good job and a comfortable career I enjoyed, it seemed like a good idea for Kevin to quit his job and try to start his own business," Erin recalled. "At first I didn't mind being the one who paid all the bills, because we both understood that after the wedding, when his business finally got going, we would have a more traditional relationship, and I'd be the one who would look forward to scaling back on work when we started a family in a few years."

"We put the baby plan on hold."

But throughout their first year, things didn't change much. The couple became more and more dependent upon Erin's salary and the benefits that were in no way negligible. And because of a sluggish economy, it didn't look as though Kevin's business would become profitable for quite some time. But instead of calling it quits or getting resentful, this couple decided to renegotiate their bargain, change some of their original plans and dreams, and adjust to that. You could call it "for poorer, for richer, for poorer for now."

"We put the baby plan on hold," Erin said. "We're both convinced that Kevin's business will make it in a few years, and we want him to have that freedom now to build for our future. So instead of continuing to rent, or buying an expensive suburban home, we bought an income-producing two-flat [a home with a rental unit] in the city, and I plan on working at least five years more before having children. Then, if necessary, we can adjust those plans too. I might look into daycare, although I hope that one day we'll be in a financial position to allow me to stay home a few years with our child." There's no ending to this couple's story, because they are, well, still negotiating—the contract and the surprises.

CHAPTER 9

Modern

Maternity

WHAT TO EXPECT WHEN YOU WANT
TO BE EXPECTING

*S*o, . . . *when are you two having kids???*

—the most annoying question asked at every wedding

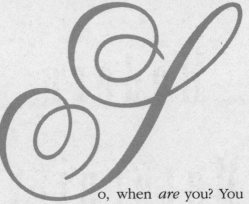

o, when *are* you? You haven't been married two hours, and people want to know: *what about kids?* Why is that? Why, suddenly, once you have been legally joined as man and wife, is your schedule of sexual intercourse a subject for public consumption?

Well, for all sorts of reasons. First, because wedding guests *think* they have a right to know! Also, because there really are only five major days in a person's life, and having your first child is one of them. People want to be in on it. (The others, of course, are [1] your "0-th" birthday—the day you were born; [2] the loss of your virginity; [3] your wedding day, which sometimes coincides with number 2; and [4] your funeral day.)

There's one other reason people ask you that question about kids so soon. Let's be honest: many of your wedding guests don't have the slightest clue what you and your spouse have been up to the last few years. That tends to limit the number of conversational topics you can comfortably share. Distant relatives can't or won't ask you about work, because they're not sure either of you has a job. Work friends don't have a clue as to who all these family members are. By asking you about your kids-to-be—when? when? when?—then, they are exercising an odd right of forced intimacy, one that happens to be bestowed upon those who return their R.S.V.P.'s on time.

Chances are, you'll even laugh the question off, in part because you don't know the answer. But also because it is a private matter at its core. Having a baby isn't something to be taken lightly, and today's brides and grooms are a little more private about this than you would expect. Especially when we find ourselves in an era in which some 50 percent of all movies are R-rated, nudity is no longer scarce on prime-time network television, and high school students have already heard everything they think they need to have heard about condoms and pregnancy.

In other cultures, having a baby together may mean a lot more to those around you than simply having gotten married. For instance, there are the Cashinahua Indians of Brazil: once a teenage girl gets permission from her father to get married, she asks her future husband to "visit her in her hammock" after her parents are asleep, writes anthropologist Helen E. Fisher in *The Anatomy of Love.* Curiously, the husband-to-be must leave, custom says, by daybreak. Gradually, though, he starts moving his things into his new family home and becomes a husband. *Except:* the marriage is *not* taken seriously until his fiancée becomes pregnant or, in the absence of that, until the marriage has lasted at least one year.[1]

Marriage Aftershocks and Pregnancy

As for your family and your family's culture, the first thing to be mindful of when it comes to pregnancy in the first year of marriage is . . . time. Just as the wedding itself—a one-day event—involved weeks and perhaps months of planning for many couples, childbearing covers a much bigger time frame in couples' lives than the proverbial nine months. As for numbers, consider that the average pregnancy lasts forty weeks; the average amount of weight gained by a new mother in the United States is twenty-seven pounds; the average cost for a normal hospital delivery is over $5,000; and if all works out as planned, the average amount of happiness and joy brought to the parents by their child is a *lifetime* of years. In other words, a baby changes the nature of a marriage in a major way, and irrevocably. Especially when it occurs in the first year of a marriage. And oftentimes, unexpected changes crop up when a planned pregnancy occurs or when a hoped-for pregnancy doesn't.

In the case of Emily and Kirk, of Stamford, Connecticut, a surprise pregnancy occurred eleven months into their marriage, and some of what Emily thought about it shocked her. "I was twenty-five when we got married," she said, "and Kirk was thirty. So he was more ready than I was." For a time, two days to be exact, Emily knew she was pregnant and didn't tell a soul—not even Kirk, who was traveling on business. She considered having an abortion and not telling her husband about that, either, but that was only a fleeting thought. Fleeting or not, it frightened her, as did other parts of the experience. However, at the time we spoke, she was a happy, giddy mother of a one-year-old boy, Martin.

"I was late with my period, which was weird in the first place, because we were using birth control," she said. "So I took a home pregnancy test—the one that gives you a plus or minus reading—and I was hanging over the stick I just peed on, waiting one minute for the whole thing to turn purple and tell me. It was a minus—meaning I wasn't pregnant. Only I *was,* I later found out. It turned out it was just too early in my pregnancy to show up on that test."

It was weird for Emily on another count, because she did the home test herself—without Kirk's help or without him watching. She hated the fact that at this point she felt she was too unsure of everything to tell him. A couple of weeks later, though, after being prescribed some antibiotics for some dental surgery, she started feeling sick and thought it was because of the medication. When the nausea persisted, she went to her doctor, told him how she felt, and that she was now seven weeks late with her period. "He said, 'I'll need to do some blood work,'" Emily recalled. Some *blood work!* "Then he came into the room and asked me: 'Do you know you're pregnant?' I was floored. I said, 'How did *that* happen?' And he said, 'If you really don't know how it happened, we'll have to make another appointment so I can explain it all to you.' I said, 'That's not funny.'"

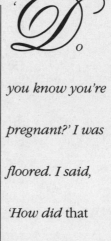

*'D*o *you know you're pregnant?' I was floored. I said, 'How did that happen?'*

Emily was scared. The first thing she thought about was an abortion. "I panicked; I don't even remember leaving the doctor's office," she said. Looking back, she remembered two thoughts from that day: One, she said to herself it was too early to have a baby, because they had not even been married a year. In her mind, that was the minimum amount of time she thought should have passed before she and Kirk would even talk about having a baby. Second, she wondered: "What would happen if he didn't want to have a child yet . . . and I did?" Because already she was wavering. She didn't want to tell her husband over the phone, and she couldn't tell any of her friends or family because her *husband* had to be the first to know.

"When he came home from his trip, he fixed a
drink," Emily said. "He started going through the mail
and I said, 'Honey, you have a bun in the oven.' It was
like he didn't hear me. 'Kirk,' I said, 'I'm pregnant.'
Then he got all excited, hugged me, jumped up and
down. He said, 'What's the matter?' because I wasn't
jumping up too. I said, 'I don't know if I'm ready for
this. I'm only twenty-five; we're not ready, financially.'
He said, 'What? I'm thirty! We're *ready*. And I'll take
care of you.'"

With that, Emily decided it felt right after all, and
they decided to have the baby for sure. They also decided to keep their little secret until a big family-and-
friends Labor Day party a week or so later. "I said to
Kirk, 'You have to tell my dad,'" Emily recalled, "'because as far as he knows, I'm a virgin!'"

When the time came for Emily's father to order the
wine at the first dinner party of the weekend (as he
does every year), Kirk cut in and cut him off. "No, I'm
going to order it," he said. "A good bottle." Then, when
the wine arrived, he made a point of filling everyone's
glass . . . except for Emily's.

"My father asked him why he didn't pour me any
wine, and that's when Kirk told my dad he was going
to be a grandfather." Nope, no wine for the pregnant
missus—the first of a nine-month series of denials, life
changes, dietary and psychological shifts that were
soon to fill her days.

All weekend from that point on, Emily practiced getting into the mind-set of being "the pregnant one." It hit
home the next day, when she was away from her family and alone with three of her girlfriends. They all
started "cracking open bottles of beer in the car," Emily
said, "and I told them, 'No thanks.'" They asked her
why she wasn't drinking, and she said because she was
pregnant. At first they didn't want to believe it, either.

"How could you do this?" they asked Emily. "This is *your* weekend," they said. "This is your *partying* weekend!"

Now the changeover was official. For the rest of the weekend, people were asking her if she felt okay; and they wouldn't let Emily clear the tables or lift stacks the likes of four plates high. "No, you rest," they said. "Don't bend over." And the reality, Emily said, was that "I was only eight and a half weeks pregnant. On my birthday three days later, I got a birthday cake with baby-bottle nipples on top next to the candles." Which sealed her transition—from newlywed to newlywed mom-to-be.

While Kirk and Emily in their first eleven months of marriage never really talked about when they were going to start trying to have children, they had talked about how *many* kids they wanted. "I wanted three," Emily said. "And he wanted point-five." "A half a kid?" I asked. "Yeah," she said. "He'd say he didn't want the bottom half, so he wouldn't have to change diapers."

A little over a year later, Emily and Kirk got a chance to catch their breath. On a Friday afternoon in fall, after they dropped Martin off with his grandparents, they headed off to San Francisco and the wine country of Sonoma County, en route to their first vacation since they had become parents. When I asked what they were going to do on their getaway, Emily didn't hesitate to answer: "Two things—we're going to sleep late every day; and have sex wherever and whenever we want. Finally." You know—the two things couples often take for granted in their first year of marriage before they think and talk too seriously about having a baby.

Adele, thirty, of Boston, is a typical newlywed bride in that she wants to wait at least one year before she gets pregnant. Like Emily used to think. "We know our relationship is going to change when kids come," Adele said. "I mean, I'll still work when I have one kid, but when the second child comes, I'll stay home. That will be a big shift for us." She and her husband, Victor, had been married just three months when we spoke.

Things, however, don't always go according to plans like this. When I listened to the story of Randi, a twenty-eight-year-old Lake Tahoe, California, housewife, and Carl, thirty-five, a previously-married father of one, I learned that in an instant. "I was twenty-two when we got married," said Randi. "But I was shocked by being pregnant. I wasn't even thinking about [getting married], to tell you the truth. It happened so suddenly.

"I took a home pregnancy test first, but it was negative [which makes you wonder, after hearing Emily's story, too, How reliable *are* these tests?]. I called Carl and told him the results, but I was crying anyway. I still felt weird for days afterward, and then I went to the doctor and found out I *was* pregnant," Randi said. "I called Carl right away, and I didn't have a lot of time to think about it. And he said, 'Let's get married.'" Randi wasn't prepared for this, but they did marry.

The situation was also complicated by the fact that Carl's daughter—a twelve-year-old from his first marriage—came to live with them, instead of with her mother, just two weeks after their wedding. So Randi was imagining, a year or two down the road, having to take care of one toddler while a teenage stepdaughter roamed the house, the neighborhood, looking for trouble the way fourteen-year-olds always seem to do.

"So we got married," Randi said, "and his daughter came to live with us." While they were also getting used to a new house, they had to think anew about Carl's ex-wife. Randi also thought she was in love, but she knows she was conflicted about things: As her pregnancy progressed, she felt she was becoming meaner, nasty even, although her husband was doing all he could to support her. "But then, I was twenty-two years old." Randi would cry now and then that first year, notably when Carl would call and talk with his ex-wife— even though they were talking about their daughter. "I'd listen in on the phone," she confessed, "and I'd think he was being too nice or somethin'. My mom said, 'What you don't know won't hurt you. Get the hell out of the room when he's talking to her!'"

Sometimes, it seems, Mother knows best. Randi and Carl ended up going to see a counselor during their first year of marriage, which helped them release some pent-up pressure, settle in and settle down. It was as if things happened so fast and furiously in their relationship, swept along by the unintended pregnancy, that they never even had time to consider going for counseling before they got married. So they opted for, and got, postmarital counseling, the kind of help that is cropping up more and more often these days, as couples and their therapists seek new ways to offer short- and long-term solutions to marriage problems without committing to six-month or year-long terms.

"I also think," Randi said, "that our kids helped us stay together during those early times. Because at the beginning of our marriage, Carl used to say things like, 'Well, maybe this just isn't *working*. Maybe we should just get a divorce.' And I'd be thinking, 'How can you say that? I want to be married forever.' He was older than me, and he was tired of putting up with other people's shit. Sometimes when we'd fight I'd even say to him that I was going to sleep on the couch." But that was *then,* she said. "It has gotten really good since," she added with a laugh. "It really has."

When Pregnancy Won't Happen

On the other end of the newlywed-pregnancy continuum, couples who wait until their mid- to late-thirties to get married and settle down don't necessarily have it easier than the likes of Randi and Carl. Listen to New York couples therapist Arden Greenspan-Goldberg, for one, who says: "I had one client who couldn't get pregnant and who found out her husband's sperm was dead." Greenspan-Goldberg, who sees clients in both New York City and nearby Westchester County, continued, "She tried artificial insemination; it didn't work (at first!). He was forty-five, she was thirty-five. And he always assumed it was his wife's medical problem.

"When she came to see me, she had been furious with him, but at the same time she *couldn't* be angry with him. 'How could I be mad at him for not giving me a child?' she'd say." And as her therapist, Greenspan-Goldberg would agree with her. But she also told her client to consider the not-so-obvious: "You're taking it out on him in different ways."

This misdirected anger is one of the most damaging consequences of pregnancy—or the lack thereof—in early married life. Whether planned or unplanned, there is often a loss of control that needs to be dealt with by both partners, or a fear of a loss of control, which in all likelihood neither of them has ever faced. The limitations imposed on a pregnant couple can be burdensome, well before they have had a chance to learn each other's style of working through conflicts, even those of a lesser nature. As Greenspan-Goldberg goes on to explain, this client of hers made some major adjustments. She in fact let her husband know how mad she was at him but also told him it *wasn't* his fault. It was venting of sorts, but directed venting.

"He didn't want to go to the doctor's to get [his sperm] tested," Greenspan-Goldberg says of the husband. "But then she told him, 'It's going to be *our* child, not your child.'" It turns out this couple went to one doctor, then to a sperm bank for consultations; they tried mightily to conceive, and finally, after three tries, they got pregnant. Was it a happy ending? Too soon to tell, but the baby was born healthy thanks to test-tube fertilization, and their story is instructive for at least two reasons: One, couples of any age, but especially those who are family oriented and marry after thirty-five or forty, should know that fertility tests and sperm counts can be performed long before the wedding. Second, there will be shocks and surprises that occur all along the pregnancy trail—not just those that afflict the mother-to-be. In this instance, as Greenspan-Goldberg says, "It's easy to be together when the sun shines." But it's the couples who come together during the troubled times that tend to end up deepening their bond.

"Before the artificial insemination worked," Greenspan-Goldberg says, "they decided to get a dog to try to ease their sadness. They were ready to try paternity leave, and it was shocking to them when it seemed he would never be able to use it. She was feeling so vulnerable, so bad, because the person she loved with all her heart was having these doubts about his masculinity. It cut into both of them deeply."

A Pregnancy "Right on Schedule"

For Geri, thirty-three, and Joel, twenty-nine, who recently married in Portland, Oregon, after dating for nine months and then being engaged for a year and a half, having a family was always a priority, although the timing of when they would have their first child didn't seem so crucial—at first.

To put it bluntly, as Geri told me, "I wasn't so hot on the idea of marriage, except for the reason of being with someone for a long time and to have children with him." She went on to say, in glowing terms, that when she met her future husband, "I did see a lot of feminine characteristics in him that would make it seem he'd be a good father." This didn't surprise me at first, until I found out that this guy who showed some of his feminine side was also a rugby player. A regular. Who plays on a team and who doesn't mind breaking a knuckle on occasion or getting tackled onto wet muddy ground now and then for the sake of a score.

"*I felt my biological clock ticking.*"

"I noticed when we were dating that he was good with women," Geri said. "A lot of my friends have said, after meeting him, that he's so respectful of women. I ended up thinking, 'This is the kind of guy who could be with me when I'm going through my emotional torques.'" As in, when she was pregnant, which she was at the time of our interview, early in her second year of marriage.

According to both Geri and Joel, who confessed to having some reservations about giving up some of their freedoms for the sake of family, they are right on schedule with their baby plans, as they both had decided they wanted to be changing diapers on their second anniversary (though of course that's not all they hoped to be doing). "I was thirty when I met Joel," Geri said. "And I felt my biological clock ticking—although it still does feel early. We haven't been married that long.

"For me," she added, "and I shouldn't speak for Joel,

I just wanted to be a *couple* for a while and have him for myself. We spend a lot of time together—some of our nicest times are sitting around the house, reading. It sounds stupid, but we're getting to where we have a natural rhythm with each other. It's almost like those nature shows on television, with the wild animals [and all their rituals]. When you have a baby, it ain't gonna be like that!"

As for their peers in marriage, studies have shown that an average of 25 percent of all couples who try to conceive will achieve this goal within one month's time. By the end of a year, between 85 and 90 percent of those trying to conceive will have succeeded.[2]

Timing isn't everything, but it is important. "I remember thinking, 'I hope we have enough time together as a couple before we become parents,'" Joel told me. "But I'm ready for the responsibility, even though it will be a shock when I see how much work is involved. Yeah," he added, "it seems a little daunting." At the same time, Geri is concerned about the loss of self-esteem she may face in terms of her career. She has worked happily as a copywriter for over seven years and is afraid that getting on the mommy track in business will hurt her prospects in the future. On the other hand, Joel pointed out that when he and Geri got engaged, he heard *all about* the constrictions of marriage; there were even "dire warnings," as he remembers them.

> "*Having a child is epic.*"

"But then," he said, "no one told me that this [marriage] was going to be the best, most joyous thing that would ever happen to us. And it is. So I'm thinking maybe it'll be the same with having a kid. Because having a child is *epic*—it's not like watching television together. And I think our foundation is so strong."

One of the biggest changes Joel noticed since his wife got pregnant was not in her stomach but in *his* brain—a protective switch clicked on. "Suddenly I'm hyperaware of who's around us," he said, "in the car or just walking in the streets. Last week, in fact, I was on a business trip in Minneapolis, and I saw a woman being harassed by a street person. I went up to help her and I shoved him—a homeless man—and then escorted her to her hotel."

Joel was apparently feeling hyperaware on the road as well as at home. And he did one other thing that's worth noting if you're pregnant and your mate's job (or yours) separates the two of you for more than a day: he bought a beeper, his first one ever. "Before I went on my trip," he said, "we learned how to use it right away, in case something happens and I need to come home right away."

Both Joel and Geri are mindful of the responsibilities they soon will face, and when they spoke with me toward the end of Geri's first trimester, they were willing to own up to some of the realities. "We already have talked about the pressures," she said. "I know I'm going to get tired. And when I do, I know I can be a pain in the ass to live with—I take it out on him. But," she added, "we did premarital counseling to look at that kind of thing. We know that the statistics are horrible about marriages that break up over the first child, and that part's very scary."

Procreational Versus Recreational Sex

There's one other facet of pregnancy that surprised Geri at first and Joel later: *trying* to get pregnant. "Sex," she said, "feels totally different without birth control. It changes the whole picture. I was on the pill for years—when the whole focus was not getting pregnant." (Geri related that she did have an abortion years ago, long before she met her husband.)

"I guess I'm a dorky Midwesterner at heart," she said, referring to her St. Louis roots, "but to have sex for the reason that you're put on the earth—that felt incredibly powerful. To *procreate*. It was sexy, for one thing. I was thinking: 'We're doing this for a reason other than Saturday afternoon fun.'"

Two months after their baby is born, Geri and Joel will likely be "doing it" for yet another reason. As childbirth expert Sheila Kitzinger points out in her helpful book, *The Year After Childbirth*, brand-new parents must first adjust to no longer being just a couple; then they must figure out a way to get their sex life back from the pregnancy or birth. Their rhythms may be upset even if the mother is able to recover quickly and have nearly pain-free intercourse eight to twelve weeks after her delivery. "They are weak and worn out," she writes of new mothers, "or they hate how their bodies look and feel after having a baby. It is as if they have been unsexed." Finally, mothers may battle for months with the fact that people will suddenly view them in an exclusively maternal role: it's as if their life before, or perhaps a lengthy career, never existed. They're suddenly Mom, Mom, Mom, Wife, Mom.

When Joel spoke of how sex has changed so far in his marriage, he didn't take a conventionally male tack. "First of all," he said, "not all sex is intercourse. And when we first started going out, we had sex for three months *without* having intercourse. It's strange, but since Geri's gotten pregnant, my sexual appetite has been the same—or increased a little bit. Hopefully that's indicative of the way things will be.

"One curious thing, though," he added a little tentatively, "is that I've gotten an incredible virile rush recently. I don't know quite how to put it, but I've been walking around, literally tumescent, a lot of the time. I had no idea this could happen. It's atavistic. I'm definitely feeling something [sexual]. Maybe it's my biological imperative." So sometimes it comes down to her clock and his imperative. Maybe Joel and Geri were just made to get married, have sex, and have babies. A lot of folks do just that. And they don't wait three years after their wedding to get going on a family, either.

Still, midway through the pregnancy they found there were some unallayed fears in their minds—fears that crop up among many pregnant newlyweds' lives. "Actually," Geri said, "I've been waking up at six in the morning thinking about things like, 'What am I going to *do* as a mother?' It's partly excitement about it, but there's an equal part of fear or panic. It's terrifying—what on *earth* makes me think I'm going to be able to be a parent?" She paused, then said, "If you ask Joel about this, he'll play it down."

Surprisingly, though, he didn't. He was, and is, mesmerized by the prospect of becoming a father. Just another beer-drinking, thoughtful, caring, sensitive rugby player, I guess.

Pregnant with No Time to Wait

Sometimes, in this era of modern maternity, the questions newlyweds ask about pregnancy have more to do with time and age than they do with the particulars of how their former lives will change. For Arlene and Warren, of Detroit, who both had been married once before they got married to each other two years ago, time was crucial. They were eager and ready to add to their family. Arlene was thirty-six and the mother of a four-year-old girl when they got engaged; Warren was forty-one and childless. Forget two years of waiting: two months after their wedding it was time to start *trying*.

Three months after the wedding, Arlene was pregnant. "We had to hurry," she said. "No joke. Once you turn thirty-five, you're considered at advanced maternal age by the health insurance companies. Sometimes they require extra tests. And Warren was ready—that's why he didn't stay with the woman he was with before me: she didn't want to have kids yet."

To be sure, women and brides over thirty-five need to know, as Arlene did, that they face higher risks (however slight) of pregnancy complications, like high blood pressure, cesarean delivery, Down's syndrome, gestational diabetes, or other conditions your doctor will no doubt tell you about. Less well known, but becoming more widely so, are the potential complications related to the father's advanced age. For instance, men over fifty-five have twice the normal risk of fathering a child with Down's syndrome that younger men do (although the risk is still quite low), and the risk of chromosomal damage in the fetus also increases with the father's age.

As for Warren and Arlene, "We have a regular sex life, and we've always had one," Arlene said. "So that wasn't a problem. It's finding time that's hard." I asked about whether they felt cheated in regard to their sex life during the pregnancy; Arlene said not at all. And she said it nonchalantly. In fact she told me: "I had sex twenty-four hours before I went to the hospital to have James."

"Is that what triggered the delivery?" I asked.

"No," she answered. "I think it was the enema."

Perhaps surprising, a regular and healthy sex life may be more important to conceiving than most people are aware, especially newlyweds who are in a hurry. According to two British researchers who studied eleven couples' intercourse habits and reported their findings in, oddly, a journal called *Animal Behaviour*, the timing of each partner's orgasm had an impact on whether or not a baby would be conceived. Women who had an orgasm from one minute before to forty-five minutes after their partner's ejaculation retained 70 to 80 percent of his sperm, the researchers found. By contrast, women who had orgasms more than one minute before their partners (or not at all) retained less than half of their partner's sperm.[3] Talk about timing! This is a tentative link, of course, since it was such a small study. But it makes you think that in this area at least, "ladies first" may not be the wisest course if baby making is on a coupling couple's mind.

Not having enough time together "just as a newlywed couple" before she got pregnant

If advancing age is what's on a couple's mind, there are a number of advantages to being an older newlywed parent, which are often overlooked. Arlene mentioned some of these—like having developed patience and a wisdom to roll with the punches—despite the fact that she also said, "It's exhausting. It's a different drain than working out at the health club or at work. You feel like you're always on alert, because [the kids] will smash their head on a slide at a McDonald's playground just when you think all is safe and under control. It's the intensity of having to protect them every minute when you're awake. Just protect, protect, and be safe. At the same time, you don't want to overdo it, because you're molding a personality."

When I told her of Geri's concern about not having enough time together "just as a newlywed couple" before she got pregnant, Arlene said, "That's for damn sure. I know exactly how she feels—because I never had that time. You do have to have time alone if you can, though, because you have to be strong enough in your relationship for when the tough stuff comes. It doesn't bother Warren as much, I think, because he was older when we got married. He's not into the hanging-out-with-the-guy-friends as much." In other words, he had the alone time throughout much of his thirties, between his first marriage and his marriage to Arlene. Enough already.

"We are not like normal people," Arlene offered. "And because it's a second marriage for both of us, we don't have groups of friends that we've gone out with for twenty years. But I have so much contact with other people, from school, Sunday school, volunteer work, part-time work, I don't necessarily *want* to be with a whole group of people on weekends, like the twenty-five-year-olds do. When I think back to when I was twenty-five—what did I do with all that time?"

It moves so much more quickly when a little one arrives.

Friendships and Friend*shifts*

Old Pals and Ex-Lover Etiquette

A groom is a bride's best friend.

—*Bride's* magazine

That should *be true!!!*

—Barb B., thirty-two, newlywed and corporate communications specialist

*C*an an old boyfriend ever really be just a friend? Can an old girlfriend? After you say, "I do," the answer is probably no. But how you as a couple handle that loaded question will tell you a lot about how you might handle the ups and downs of dealing with your *other* friends. Remember: when you say your vows, you *take* a husband or wife for life. With friends it's different; you *make* them only if you're lucky.

Of all the questions that arise about friends after marriage, the ones that stir up the most debate—if not exactly trouble—are those that concern friends of the opposite sex. And it's not just old boyfriends or girlfriends that kick up conflict. Consider: should a wife continue to go out to lunch every once in a while with her two best male friends from when she was single? If you say yes, then for how long? Likewise, should a husband keep in touch, maybe go out for drinks, with one or two of his female friends from his bachelor days? Again, for how long? Months? Years? You might also ask yourself why these buddies are known as friends of the "opposite sex"—an intriguing phrase. Is it because there is, inevitably, at least a *hint* of sexual tension or attraction in the relationship? (We all know that opposites attract.) Or is that just an instinctive fear that gets played out too vocally, too obviously, too often?

Before these questions are answered, it's important for you and your spouse to admit something about your opposite-sex friends: at one time, there *was* some attraction that occurred between you or your spouse and those friends. At the same time, however, these attractions were not necessarily sexual. Or even flirtatious. They may have been, sure, but they may also have been attractions that had to do with a friend's sense of humor. Just as likely, they may have sprung from a friend's sense of openness that was inviting and more frank than that which came from friends of the same sex. Finally, the attractions of opposite-sex friends may have stemmed from a psychological lift of sorts—they may have sent signals to you or your spouse that said, yes, you are indeed attractive to others should your present relationship(s) not work out.

Now for the tough part: these feelings of attraction were and are real, and they deserve to be acknowledged in view of how you as a couple will handle the inevitable fallout from them. It's easy to dismiss them. It's not so easy to own up to them. But if you do, you may find it worth your while.

"I think couples need to put their cards on the table early on," says Bryan Brook, Ph.D., a couples counselor and marital therapist in Denver. "If a wife has some close male friends, or if a husband has close female friends, that person needs to say to his spouse: 'This person means a lot to me.' I call it a 'sexclusive relationship.'" Brook, who writes and lectures often on the subject of "designer marriages," isn't just being cute with a quote when he talks about "sexclusive" this and "sexclusive" that. He believes that there's a place for these relationships, these friendships, in marriage as long as they are honestly placed in context. In Brook's view, one crucial question that needs to be asked and answered by both husband and wife is this: *Is either of you going to resent the other for having to give up time you used to spend with good friends, especially those of the opposite sex?*

It's tough for many newlyweds to honestly say no. So what do they do? They avoid the question.

"When you lose one of your best friends," Brook says, "it's almost like a divorce. Think about it: you might be getting married and at the same time asked to divorce your best friend. You betcha that gets acted out! But these things need to be acted out *prior* to the marriage. It has nothing to do with sex; if you can't trust someone to spend time with one of their best friends, then you probably shouldn't be marrying that someone."

In a somewhat softer tone, Sandra Jones-Pollack, Ph.D., a couples therapist in Granby, Connecticut, suggests, "If you have a rewarding platonic friendship with a man and that person is special to you, it's important to keep it when you marry—just like it's important to see your female friends."[1]

I wondered if what Brook and Jones-Pollack believe squared with what other marital counselors might think, so I thumbed through some phone book–sized bridal magazines one day and came across a telling page from a recent issue of *BRIDE'S*. A tremulous fiancée had written to the editors: "My fiancé keeps in touch with one of his ex-girlfriends. He plans to invite her to our wedding and to remain friendly with her after he and I are married. I am trying to be understanding . . . but . . . should I object to the friendship?"[2]

It was a tough question, to be sure, so the editors asked not one or two experts for advice on this matter but *four* of them. And, perhaps surprising, they pretty much agreed not to freeze out the ex.

"Absolutely not," this is not objectionable, said expert number one, Michael S. Broder, Ph.D., author of the book *The Art of Staying Together.* "The fact that he is marrying you gives testimony that you're the one he's chosen." Besides, Broder added, this groom-to-be was handling this openly and honestly: if the ex is interested in still seeing him, that might also mean this guy's treated the women in his past rather well.

"Your jealous feelings show that you do object, so express these feelings," said expert number two, Jane G. Goldberg, Ph.D., author of *The Dark Side of Love.* She added, though, that talking about these feelings is different from acting on them. In other words, no "threats or ultimatums." Goldberg's final judgment: a compromise could work here. The fiancé might scotch the wedding invite to his ex; if so, his betrothed shouldn't object to an occasional phone call or lunch meeting.

Opposite-sex friends are necessary for a healthy life.

"You need other friends—and opposite-sex friends are necessary for a healthy life," advised expert number three, Cranor Graves, author of *Building a Better Marriage.* He went on to explain that if you let a fiancé know you trust him, chances are that he'll more likely *be* trustworthy.

By saying, in short, "It depends," expert number four put it all together. James Vaughan, Ph.D., author of *Making Love Stay,* explained that "there is a big difference between a long-term relationship that ended just before you two became involved and a few casual dates." Vaughan said that, in either case, it would be fair to ask the groom-to-be to include his fiancée/wife in the future meetings. But at the same time, if it was a longtime girlfriend, he should hear, from his bride or a knowing other, that it will eventually put a strain on his relationship with his wife. Starting with the wedding day. Delay not; cross her off the list.

So that's what the experts said. Fair enough. But I went to some other experts—newlyweds who didn't have books to sell—to see how they had handled this kind of situation when it came up early in their marriages. As you'll see, their answers aren't nearly so neat and tidy. Because, if you want to know the truth, neither is newlywed life when you try to mesh friends into the already crowded mix of husband, wife, in-laws, work, moving, housecleaning, cooking, maybe house hunting, and, of course, hobbies for all your free time.

"Jack doesn't have any female friends," says Hennie, twenty-five, a San Diego, California, high school teacher. "He would never invite a woman to lunch, and he's very offended when a man calls me."

This sounded like a dangerous reaction when I heard it during our interview (Jack was at work at the time), and I wondered if I was missing part of her answer or part of this couple's story. When I pressed Hennie to elaborate, she didn't hesitate.

"He thinks that men always want *more,*" she said. "It's kind of ironic; he has a very feminine side to him." In saying this about her husband, she was implying that he isn't as closed up as a lot of men she knows. "He sees his male friends one-on-one; they are a lot like he is," she added. "They'll talk about one issue for hours! But it'll usually be something about economics or politics, not about personal matters. Except," that is, "with his best friend (and best man).

"We got married last August," Hennie added, "and I had lost four [male] friends already." She was speaking about a time span of ten months in which her roster of male friends dwindled from rather full to next to nothing.

"You're friends with someone because you're attracted to them," Hennie explained rather frankly. "When I got married, I was now considered unavailable to them. Some men, when they become your friends, may think: hey, five years down the road, maybe there will be more than friendship. When I think back on it, a *lot* of them made sexual advances toward me."

She mentioned one male friend whom she met in college on the East Coast who disappeared "all of a sudden" when he found out she was getting married. "You want to marry your best friend—and he might even be a good lover—but I knew the combination just wasn't there with [this disappearing friend]," Hennie said.

Truth be told, even for millions of married couples, the combination Hennie speaks of just *isn't* there. It's not that friendship dampens sexual desire or that it makes sex seem stale. It has more to do, I think, with what marital therapists like Terry Real of the Family Institute near Boston brought up back in Chapter 6: that marriage involves a partnership filled with roles; that your spouse is not only your partner for life—your husband or wife—but also your protector, your confidant, your provider (at times), your personal accountant/money manager/tax planner, your maid (at times), and, most times, your best friend. So is it really fair, then, to blame a potential dampening of sexual desire on the sole fact that you may have married your best friend? I don't think so. Neither do the couples counselors like Real who handle these kinds of questions on a daily basis.

Kirsten, thirty-two, who has been married barely a year and who works two days a week in her husband, Don's, family's grocery store in northern California, said things have been noticeably different with her friends since she became a wife. "I had some male acquaintances, who I saw when I went to the gym a lot," she said. "They were usually professionals, attorneys, you know, and I wondered whether maybe there was some other innuendo there. I mean, we all have some behavior that's like animals. . . . But they kind of stopped calling. It's too bad for them.

"Don had a tighter group of friends than I did since he grew up around here," she added. "I moved to the area when I started my own consulting business. Even his ex-girlfriend lived in one of his houses."

Hold it right there. His ex-girlfriend was a tenant in one of his houses? And his then fiancée saw nothing wrong with that? Actually, she did: it felt like unfinished business. But she didn't say anything to Don about it *at first*. She let time pass, and at the same time the lease ran out. Then, when she figured she had been understanding enough, she asked her husband whether it wouldn't be a good idea to look for another tenant for the property. It was as if to say, but not actually voice the words: "It's over, Don. Why don't we let it be over *for good?*" Yes, Don was still friends with his ex-girlfriend, but he needn't be her landlord anymore to keep the friendship going. And as it happened, the friendship faded, without a blowup or major confrontation. It just took patience on Don and Kirsten's part, and one slightly intimidating visit to the ex's home by Kirsten. Fortunately for both of them, there was no shortage of tenants looking for affordable housing in this desirable northern California community to replace the ex as tenant. So that part was easy.

"I learned, in a situation like this," Kirsten said, "to say what you feel and to be patient. But also say what you have to say and yet never disrespect the person you're talking about." By using restraint in both her language and her manner, Kirsten was able to defuse a

potentially touchy situation in which her husband
might be pressed to defend his ex-girlfriend or to defend his business reasons for allowing her to remain in
the house *they* now owned.

"I allowed it to go on for two years," Kirsten recalled,
"and finally he told me that it wasn't even really a
friendship. He said they'd talk about the rent and whatever, and then they'd talk about friends we all had in
common. One day I went down to the house to say,
'Hi,' and she said, 'I think it's time I moved out.'"

When you hear tales like this one, you tend to think
that the rules of ex-lover etiquette (if there are indeed
such rules) haven't yet made the rounds. According to
the folks who would be expected to know such things,
like Elizabeth L. Post, author of *Etiquette,* the rules are
simple: "Lunch once," she says, "dinner never." Over
and out. Judith Martin, better known to newspaper
readers across America as Miss Manners, agrees that a
lunch meeting with an ex–boyfriend or girlfriend
would be okay but suggests it be a lunch for three:
with you, your ex, and your spouse in attendance.[3]

Friends of Your Own

In a similar vein, the question of spending time with
your own friends apart from your spouse will inevitably arise early in your marriage. One wife I spoke
with, Lorna, thirty-two, of Portland, Oregon, thought
about her first few months and said she remembered
feeling guilty, confused, and thought to herself, "Wait a
minute—these are my *friends* . . . I didn't think it was
gonna be like this!"

"The hardest part," she said, "was not asking permission, but having Tom say, 'Well, are you really going
out again?'

"For us, checking in was calling to say that I was going to be late; I really don't go out that much anymore
[now that they are in their second year of marriage],
but it was a big adjustment at first—the first year. I
would get all dressed up and I was going out, and Tom
was like, 'You're wearing *that* without me?' or, 'Every
guy is gonna be all *over* you!' It wasn't that he didn't
trust me: he didn't trust everybody else; that kind of
thing. Back then it was an issue."

But it isn't, fortunately, anymore.

"I think it bothered him when I went out with my
girlfriends," she said, "because he really didn't have too
many guys to go out with. He had one friend, where I
had a whole bunch of friends, and I still went out at
least twice a week with my girlfriends."

Sometimes people compromise a friendship to please their mate.

Problem was, Lorna had to call in and
check in with Tom more often than she
liked. "Yeah," she said, "if I called him and
I was drunk, or at the time I was still partying—and he's so against that—I would be
afraid, or I'd lie. I did some lying the first
year."

It was lying born out of a fear of conflict—conflicts that did occasionally arise
but eventually faded out between their
sixth and eighteenth months of marriage.

"Sometimes people compromise a friendship to please
their mate," therapist Bryan Brook says, "and then a hidden resentment sets in. They think they're doing the
right thing, but in fact they're compromising part of their
heart, their self. And that gets played out—not uncom-
monly with an affair. It's as if a partner says, 'I gave up
this, or that, and you're not gonna control me. I'll show
you!'" In his own personal life (he is once divorced) as
well as in some of his counseling sessions, Brook finds it
helpful for couples to set up specific boundaries that

have to do with friends, finances, and the concept of monogamy—especially in the age of AIDS. He believes that putting commitments down on paper can improve a relationship, perhaps even free it up a bit, despite the fact that many partners would view such documents and partnership agreements as overly clinical.[4]

Kim, thirty-two, a traditionally raised Southerner with Baptist influences in her family, told me she had a difficult time at first when it came to dealing with friendships and marriage—and trust. Now in her second year of marriage, she said there were times when her husband, Reid, would go out with his male friends and he wouldn't always make it home until after daybreak the next morning. He'd be too drunk to drive, he'd say, or too wiped out to travel if he and his friends didn't stop partying until five in the morning. In this year of their marriage, he has still gone out all night with the guys at times, but less often than in the first months after he and Kim married. As he tells it, Reid actually gave up his friends for a while—six months or so—right after the wedding. Now, when he sees them and stays up all night drinking and playing pool, he and Kim have a deal: they have a curfew, which is sunrise, no matter which of them is out with the pals. It might seem extremely *late* to many couples—sunrise as a curfew— and dangerous, but for Kim and Reid it works. One reason may be that they honestly do trust each other. Even into the wee hours of the morning.

Secondly, on his earlier nights out, she said Reid can't just come home and crash into bed. "If he can stay out until midnight with his friends," she allowed, "he can come home and talk with me."

"She won't be mad," Reid added, sounding a little surprised as he said it. "She just wants to *talk*. I used to go out a lot until six or seven in the morning when I was single. But I feel I can do it once in a while now *because* we are married. I'm not out chasing skirts, and she knows that. I say to my friends, 'Hey guys, I gotta be home by sunup.' A lot of guys I know wouldn't tell their friends that. But I love her."

Clear across the country, Don, who runs the grocery store in northern California, sounded a little more grounded when he talked about himself and his wife, Kirsten, and their time out with friends. "She had fewer friends [here in town] than I did when we got engaged," he said. "So she basically jumped into my world, with my friends. Of course she had relationships before, as I did, and I met one of her ex-boyfriends—it turns out I went to grade school with him. But we both have such a strong opinion of ourselves, we started from a great position."

At the risk of sounding too confident, maybe even cocky, Don cleared up any possible misconception: "What I mean was, we were ready to settle down together. We were totally able to live alone, but we weren't necessarily looking for that. We had a lot of security within ourselves." And, he added, there was a sense of security they got from their friends, no matter what their gender happened to be. As for the potential for jealousy between them and their opposite-sex friends, Don said, "I don't think either of us was ever looking over our shoulders to check up on the other. We've always been surrounded by people; we like social intensity. So, if anything, we find ourselves looking for excuses to find times for *ourselves,* just the two of us, without friends in the picture." When Don told me this, he did so almost apologetically, as if he were hurting his friends—slighting them with his honesty. The truth is, he and Kirsten are easygoing, energetic, attractive, focused, professional, and fun people who would not surprisingly draw more than a few calls a week from friends interested in getting together this weekend. Or next.

After reviewing his and Kirsten's last few weeks of time with friends, Don realized that Kirsten does have a couple of close friends that she met through their family business, and that these might even be considered more her friends than his. "There's one guy who talks with her a lot and who needs a lot of maintenance," Don said, meaning she provides the support and attention. "And a lot of guys would have problems with that. But I don't."

Think about it, he explained: if the person you're committed to spend the rest of your life with is worth her salt, then you've got to face the fact that there are going to be guys who are going to approach her—under the guise of business, or friendship, or both. And there is only one way to handle that situation: "You've gotta put a hundred and ten percent of your trust into that person you've decided to marry," Don said. "Jealousy is such a waste of time. I'm not saying that I'm incapable of feeling it, because I have. But maybe because I [waited and] got married at thirty-three instead of a decade earlier, I can handle it better."

As for his own friends, things really didn't change much during his first year of marriage, largely because of the hectic pace he keeps with work and rehab projects at home—building a deck and a spa in the backyard—projects he prefers to do on his own time with his own hands. His best friend was also his best man, and they continue to see each other an average of once a week, usually for a mountain bike ride in the hilly regions of Marin County, where they've both lived for years. Sure, it's true that he'd like to spend more time with his best buddy. But Don is perceptive enough to know that it was life that got in the way of some of his friendships, not marriage. And not everybody

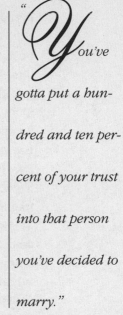

"You've gotta put a hundred and ten percent of your trust into that person you've decided to marry."

is able to make that subtle but important distinction.

I found it interesting that when Don talked about his best friend and their lack of time together, he mentioned work pressures, home projects, and then their weekly bike rides. Are these normal, healthy newlywed-male priorities? Normal, yes, but not *necessarily* healthy, believes Herb Goldberg, Ph.D., a prominent Los Angeles therapist who specializes in men's issues. For despite a long camaraderie or seemingly deep friendship, men's personal interactions often remain fragile underneath.

"Most men have 'activity friends,'" he explains, "men who are extensions of their interests in sports such as tennis, golf, football, or in other external interests. When the activity is absent, the pleasure in and reasons for continuing the relationship usually dissolve." Goldberg adds, rather pessimistically I would say, that marriage tends to offer a reason for men to close off friendships more frequently than it does for women. "As men get older," he writes, "they become more withdrawn from personal relationships."[5] This may be a helpful thing for the aforementioned Kim to ponder while she awaits the return of her night-owl partner the next time he heads out to party with his friends.

Five Questions to Ask About Friends

If you can answer these questions with your fiancé or spouse openly and honestly, experts say, you are on a good course in regard to your friends and your first year of marriage.

1. Should you (did you) invite your ex-boyfriend/ex-girlfriend to the wedding? Was the decision painstaking or difficult?

2. Will lunches with old girlfriends/boyfriends be allowed once you're married? How about meetings for drinks? Dinner?
3. Is a weekly or monthly girls'/boys' night out okay?
4. What if a friend asks you to keep secret, for example, an affair or abortion? Would you tell your spouse? Always?
5. How many *really* good friends does your spouse have? How does that number compare with yours?

On the flip side, some wives worry more about their husbands accepting their longtime female friendships. "There aren't any of Jack's friends that grate on me," Hennie, of San Diego, said, "but there are a few of mine that he considers nettlesome."

What does she mean by "nettlesome"? Untimely phone calls, for starters. "When you're calling someone who's married," she said, "there's an etiquette involved. For us, you probably shouldn't call after eight at night, and don't call on a Saturday morning or on Sunday." Her husband's frenzied Wall Street–type work hours are such that when he's off work and not traveling (which he frequently does), he wants to enjoy uninterrupted time with his wife. "He's very 'When it's our time, it's *our* time,'" Hennie said. "He's resentful of friends who don't get that; he'll say, 'Get off the phone—I'm home now.' We don't even pick up the phone when he's home."

It's not clear whether Hennie buys into this "don't call" etiquette wholeheartedly, but she's willing to espouse it, for now at least, for her marriage's and her friends' benefit. "I start calling people at seven P.M.," she said, which makes one realize why friendships are harder to maintain in today's harried times. For if these rules of newlywed phone etiquette are obeyed, that means the hours after 8 P.M. and a good chunk of weekends are off-limits for calls from friends. This would leave workday hours or those right after dinner Monday through Friday as allowable phone time—that is, *if* dinner is eaten promptly at six each weeknight.

Single Versus Married Friends

. In many newlyweds' households, over a matter of months, an evolution takes place in which single friends seem to lose their place in favor of married couples—or at least those who are borderline, maybe living together. It's not so much a conscious freeze-out of old friends but more a time when similar sensibilities just start to seem more comfortable for the newly married. Sometimes what happens is that one spouse realizes that he or she has more friends nearby, and it doesn't seem fair if the other spouse doesn't.

For example, Anne and Larry, of Dundee, Illinois, took stock of their single-to-married-friend ratio and found it, well, not equal. "I think I have a closer circle of friends around me, more so than Larry," said Anne, twenty-six. "I have a couple of friends who used to be my roommates, and we're pretty tight. We'll get together once in a full moon, and it's pretty intimate, despite the fact that some time has passed." For better or worse friendships, however, Anne has made sure to invite Larry to these nights out, so he can come along if he wants to. "I think he feels pretty welcomed," she said, "but it's interesting: I'm the first in my circle of friends to get married."

What's notable about Anne inviting her husband into her circle of single friends was that she seemed surprised that things have gone so smoothly. When asked what she thought newlyweds were most likely to fight about, she said, "friends." (For his part, Larry said the best times they have spent together as newlyweds were "being by ourselves.") In addition, Anne compared her friends' reactions to her husband joining them to the feelings that sometimes surface when brothers and sisters react to a new love interest in the family. "It's like when your siblings don't reassure you when they don't like the person you're dating," Anne said. "You wonder what's going on. I actually have nine brothers and sisters, and let me tell you, even if I didn't give a damn about sibling approval, I got my share of it! They make sure they're looking out for the others."

As for Larry, he said that getting married, changing jobs, and moving all in a matter of months combined to cut him off from his closest friends. "The friendships I have that are really strong are with the people I've known for a while, starting back in college. And we're kind of scattered, so we don't spend the time together that we used to. (Now it's maybe a few times a month.) What's happened, over time, is that my work relationships have developed into work friendships." But they aren't as close-knit as his relationships with his former best friends—not by a long margin. When asked whether any of his single male friends now feel cut off from him due to his being married, Larry didn't hesitate two seconds. "Not in the least bit," is all he said.

Another newly married husband, Brent, a doctor from outside of Milwaukee, reported that sometimes his male friends will invite him out and say, "Tell Jane to come along," whether or not they actually mean it.

He usually doesn't bring her along. "I'm like, 'Oh, she won't be able to make it,'" Brent said. "It's no big deal—I think they may be feeling guilty that they're taking me away from her, but you know, Jane understands. And I understand. I want her to go out with her girlfriends, go out to dinner, gossip about college days, whatever."

In a quieter moment, Brent finally will admit that sometimes "when I'm watching a game at home on TV, I'd rather be with the guy friends." Guilt happens; then he catches himself. "But neither of us are possessive in that way," he added. The only problem here, marital therapists would say, is that he is perhaps overcompensating for feeling possessive about his friends and time; in other words, worrying about being selfish. In fact, couples counselors will tell you, it isn't selfish.

As careful readers of *BRIDE'S* would have learned back in 1987, newlyweds are often excessively protective of each other and their relationships. This, in turn, can result in one partner monopolizing the other's time and energy—which is about the time that friends, especially single friends, can start to feel like sudden strangers. "If the bride thinks she's in the power position because she's married, and that a friend is the underdog because she's not [married]," believes Claudia Schweitzer, a family therapist in Gloucester, Massachusetts, "then that's going to be detrimental."[6]

Kim, the thirty-two-year-old Southerner, pointed out to me that some of Reid's single friends, who tease him about calling her to say he'll be late coming home, probably do so because they don't *have* anyone to go home to. Nor do they have someone to check in with late at night when worrying would otherwise click in. Come sunup, as often as not, these single guys are alone.

Shared Friends

Unlike material possessions that both spouses bring to a new household, friendships born of past histories and shared experiences don't automatically meld once you take your vows. The two of you may both *agree* that you'd like to share your friends completely, but as Brian McDonald, an oft-quoted New York City psychotherapist, likes to say, "Just because you think it's so doesn't mean it's so." As an example, listen to one newlywed quoted in a recent issue of *Modern Bride:* "From the time I graduated from college," she said, "I felt like I was missing out on so many things because I wasn't married. I never went out of my way to make friends . . . so I rarely had any fun. I also felt sure that if I had a husband, things would be different. There just seemed to be this enormous void that needed to be filled to make me feel useful and worthwhile."[7] When her husband's friends (of whom there were many) failed to adopt her instantly, however, she was both surprised and hurt.

To the contrary, Brent, the doctor who has been married one year, says it hasn't been nearly so hard to merge his and his wife's friends. Perhaps it's because they are both outgoing types with easygoing personalities. "We both go out with friends separately sometimes," Brent said, "and sometimes we go out together. In fact, Jane sometimes worries that I don't spend enough time with my friends. I would say about both of us that about half of our friends are married and half are single."

When asked how his wife manages the friends department of their marriage, Brent didn't hesitate: "She's like, 'Oh, you haven't gone out with whomever in a couple of weeks,' or whatever. She definitely encourages that, although it's not like I'm out hangin' with the guys every weekend." At this point Brent sounded a tad defensive.

"Most of the time when we go out, I'm with her. And about twice a month, I go out with just the guys. I have about three friends who I hang out with for the most part, whom I'll go out with by myself—watch a basketball game or something. My wife is really easygoing, though. She likes basketball, for instance, and she can talk about anything, and she's comfortable being around my guy friends. I'd say about four times a month we go out—with all our friends—together. Like either Jane with my friends, or I go with her and some of her friends." Which, when you think about it, is about as balanced as you could get and still have some sense of independence outside of the marriage as well as within it.

Tere, forty-two, of Minneapolis, in the first year of her second marriage (she has two children from her first marriage; her husband has one), said that her stage in life pretty much dictates that she and her husband, Jim, spend most of their friends time with couples. Not that children force them into this; it has more to do with age.

"We're going on vacation with a set of Jim's friends that he introduced me to," Tere said, "and we get together with other couples that I know—and then we have our own sets. He will do things with his buddies, and I will do things with some of my single girlfriends, and we won't necessarily share those experiences. It wouldn't be obnoxious [to do so], we just don't do it. It's just that some of our friends are just acquaintances, like the guys that Jim plays hockey with. There's also some people from my job at the bakery I get together with for lunch—but I wouldn't drag Jim in on it. Because there would be nothing that we'd have in common. We base a lot of our social activities on family."

Lorna and Tom, from Portland, have merged their friends to an even greater degree. "Tom's friends are mostly all my friends," Lorna said. "He hangs out with my friends, and that's because he's gotten really athletic, which my friends happen to be. His friends were more computer-type kinds of people, very business oriented. It was kind of weird: we'd get together, and I can be real loud and outgoing and obnoxious. And his friends were very quiet, more like Tom. But Tom's personality changed once he started hanging around with me and my family and my friends. It was like a personality that was dying to come out."

Did his friends just disappear?

"Well, a lot of them," she explained. "Like Tom, they didn't have a lot of real close friends either. In Tom's case, it was also because his girlfriend before me was clingy with him. She didn't drive; she didn't do anything for herself; she relied on Tom for everything." According to Lorna, Tom told her that he lost a lot of his friends because of his last girlfriend's behavior and insecurity.

Happily, he ended up gaining a lot of friends through his wife, even though there was some trepidation at first: at times, one of Lorna's female friends, Christina, would overpower Tom with her bluster and her outgoing personality. Tom would actually leave the house, protesting that he would never be that rude. He'd say, "Well, I'm going to go wash my car; I'm going to vacuum my car." Meanwhile, Lorna thought perhaps her friends had shocked him with their frank talk about sexual this and sexual that. Growing up, Tom didn't have any sisters, so when he heard Lorna's friends open up and really *talk,* he didn't have anything to compare it to. He didn't realize that a lot of women talk like that when they get together. Nowadays, he is not what you'd call raunchy when they all get together, but

"*He* hangs out with all my friends."

he is more tolerant. (Lorna says she thinks he actually enjoys the candor of some of these friendly encounters.)

"Nowadays," Lorna said about Tom, "he hangs out with all my friends. And if Christina calls now when I'm not home or even if I am home, they'll talk on the phone for like forty-five minutes, or he'll go over and visit with her."

While it sometimes hits home too hard, one often overlooked question you or your mate might consider in regard to your friends is, How much should you change in regard to making new friends brought into your life by your mate? There are fuzzy lines between sharing friends, tolerating them, splitting them up, and simply keeping in contact with them. But in terms of your development as a couple and as individuals, the lines are worth navigating. As Susan Page says in her book *Now That I'm Married, Why Isn't Everything Perfect?*: "Couples who thrive build fences, not fortresses. They balance their time, their space, their work, their money, their secrets, and their emotional responsibilities carefully between 'mine' and 'ours.'"[8] They also, it seems clear by now, balance their friends.

To be sure, there's one last point to consider about friends and marriage: if after a year of marriage you find yourself with two or three fewer friends than you had before you were engaged, it's not necessarily the case that marriage sabotaged the friendships. Chances are, if you had remained single, you would similarly have noticed the number of good friends of yours dwindling with the passage of years. The fact is, time does that to friends with or without marriage entering the picture. And those who realize this before the wedding will be better able to handle the discomfort that accompanies these shufflings of friendships—you

could even call them "friend*shifts*"—during the first
twelve months of your marriage. But just remember,
from your wedding day forward, you're going to count
on having a good friend at your side. Like none you've
had before.

$\mathcal{A}$fterword

It wasn't just another credit card call.

It was six forty-five in the morning in Chicago's O'Hare Airport, a wintry December day with snow-banks on the runway, and a young man about thirty years of age, in a sport jacket and tie, stood at a pay phone at Gate H-8, awaiting his announcement to board. I saw a wedding ring on his finger, and while I was on hold two phones away, I eavesdropped on his conversation. "Leave it on my voice mail. I'll be back on Friday," he said in businesslike tones, and hung up.

He then made another call and his voice changed. I heard him talk softly, sweetly. "Hi, Hon," he said, "I didn't want to wake you. I was hoping to get the machine. I just wanted to tell you that Davy Jones is going to be on the Loop [a Chicago rock 'n' roll radio station] from seven to nine, talking about *Grease*. . . . Go back to sleep, Hon. I love you. Buh-bye."

This phone call made me feel good about marriage. After talking with nearly a hundred husbands and wives over the course of fifteen months, I came to appreciate the little things newlyweds—and those *not* so newly wed—do for each other, like sharing news of radio interviews with washed-up pop star Monkees à la Davy Jones, or making coffee or tea *just* the way their spouse likes it, or remembering the funky little anniversaries (first date, first fight, first day on the job) as well as the big ones.

With his quick little phone call, the husband I heard that morning at O'Hare found a way to share something with his wife even while they were apart, however corny it might have been. That's love, that's marriage, that's the kind of stitch, I believe, that will go a long way toward firming up the seams of a good, solid marriage. I can't prove it, of course. Neither can the experts.

Not having strong ties and relationships, including marriage, constitutes a major risk factor to one's health.

But I can optimistically point out the good work of sociologist James S. House, Ph.D., of the University of Michigan, who reviewed studies of more than seven thousand men and women and found that *not* having strong ties and relationships, including marriage, constitutes a major risk factor to one's health. Dr. House feels so strongly about this that he believes quickie divorces should be outlawed—and that preventive premarital counseling might be made mandatory.[1] Not surprising, he is also a fan of marital therapy—even though he is not a therapist himself. Good relationships make for good health; little things couples do for each other, over months and years, make for good marriages.

I'm also pleased to report that the same week I heard the Chicago man's Davy Jones phone call, Cheryl Lavin, a relationships columnist for the *Chicago Tribune,* published a handful of letters from readers who wrote in to challenge the notion of social scientists who say, in short, that "crazy in love" doesn't last much past the first or second anniversaries.

"This morning, while changing our bedding, I stopped, held my husband's pillow to my face, and inhaled his fragrance," one woman, who had been married fourteen years, wrote. Another, a wife of nine years, said of her husband, "He still pats my behind, puts his arms around me, hugs me for no reason except that he loves me."

No reason for a hug? I'd say that "except that he loves me" is a pretty big reason. And it is one final lesson for newlyweds to take along on the road—if not quite forever, then at least well into your second year of marriage.

Appendix

As a way to supplement the seventy-five in-person interviews conducted for *Your First Year of Marriage*, I distributed more than 150 copies of the following survey across the United States.

Survey Questionnaire
YOUR FIRST YEAR OF MARRIAGE

This informal survey about love and marriage is designed to do two things:

(1) gather a wide variety of women's and men's honest views about the early stages of marriage, and (2) help thousands of newlywed and other couples cope with issues that neither partner was (or is) quite prepared for when they got (or get) married. Your responses will be on a first-name basis only and will supplement scores of in-person interviews that will be summarized in a book to be published by Fireside/Simon & Schuster in 1995.

The author is Curtis Pesmen, who wrote *How a Man Ages* and *What She Wants: A Man's Guide to Women* for Ballantine Books, New York, in 1984 and 1992. Please answer the questions you're comfortable with and mail the survey to the author.

Curtis Pesmen
c/o Fireside Books/Simon & Schuster
Rockefeller Center
1230 Avenue of the Americas
New York, NY 10020

Thank you for your help and input!

INTRODUCTORY INFORMATION

(PLEASE PRINT)

FIRST NAME: _____

LAST INITIAL (OPTIONAL): _____

HOME CITY/STATE (OR REGION, E.G., MIDWEST): _____

GENERAL CAREER FIELD: _____

RELIGION (OPTIONAL): _____

MARITAL STATUS/NUMBER OF YEARS OR MONTHS: _____

AGE ____ NUMBER OF TIMES MARRIED_____

NUMBER OF TIMES LIVED WITH A PARTNER OUTSIDE

OF MARRIAGE_____

QUESTION 1

Is it easier or harder to make marriage work today
than it was for your parents? _____

Why?_____

_____

_____

QUESTION 2

Are honeymoons underrated, overrated, or neither,
in your opinion? _____

Why?_____

_____

_____

QUESTION 3

What two or three issues are MOST important to a
couple in the first year of marriage? _____

_____

_____

_____

QUESTION 4

For newlyweds, what do you think are the activities that bring them the most pleasure? _____

_____

_____

QUESTION 5

What do you think newlyweds are most likely to fight about in the first year of marriage (for example, in-laws, money, friends, sex, chores)? _____

_____

_____

QUESTION 6

When should a wife and husband decide how they will divide the household duties? _____

_____

_____

QUESTION 7

Do you think the first few years of marriage are easier for couples in their twenties or those who got (or get) married in their thirties or forties? Or sixties? _____

_____

_____

Why? _____

_____

_____

QUESTION 8

For couples married a long time, what do you think are the activities that might bring them the most pleasure or satisfaction? _____

_____

_____

QUESTION 9

In your opinion, is it important that a couple have sex often in their first year of marriage? If so, why and how often? _____

_____

_____

QUESTION 10

Do you think premarital couples counseling or psychotherapy is wise, essential, or a waste of time for most engaged couples? _____

Why? _____

_____

_____

QUESTION 11

What about love is most essential to good marriage: friendship, intimacy, trust, or passion? _____

Why? _____

_____

_____

QUESTION 12

In your opinion, is it feasible for a couple in love to wed if one partner wants badly to have children and the other is strongly against the idea? _____

_____

_____

QUESTION 13

It is estimated that half of all married men have sex with other partners; the rate is becoming similar for women. Can you envision a case where a newlywed has an affair and the marriage survives?

_____

_____

_____

QUESTION 14

Who in your opinion has more unrealistic expectations of marriage: women or men?_____

Why?_____

_____

_____

Thanks again for your time and contributions!

If you'd like to volunteer for a follow-up interview or to suggest couples for interview, please fill in your phone number: _____/_____

For more information about *Your First Year of Marriage,* write:

Editor

Fireside Books/Simon & Schuster

1230 Avenue of the Americas

New York, NY 10020

(212) 698-7000

Notes

Chapter 3

1. Karen Peterson, *USA Today,* October 11, 1993, D1–2.
2. Nitya Lacroix, *Massage for Lovers* (London: Carlton Books Ltd.; San Francisco: HarperCollins Publishers), 46.

Chapter 4

1. Marty Klein, Ph.D., "Sexual Secrets: Should You Bare All?" *Modern Bride,* August/September 1994, 46.
2. W. W. Meade. "The M-Word We Dare Not Say," *Cosmopolitan,* April, 1993, 208.
3. William Betcher, M.D., "Secrets of Intimacy," *Self,* August 1994, 106–7.

Chapter 5

1. Editors of BRIDE'S magazine, *Wedding Nightmares* (Plume Press, 1993). Chapter on "Objections and Altarcations," pp. 145–46.
2. Penny Bilofsky and Fredda Sacharow, *In-Laws/Outlaws* (Copestone Press/Fawcett, 1991), 13.
3. Maggie Scarf, *Intimate Partners* (New York: Ballantine Books, 1987), 36.

Chapter 6

1. Mark Clements, "Sex in America Today," *Parade,* August 7, 1994, 4.
2. Philip Elmer-Dewitt, "Now for the Truth About Americans and Sex," *Time,* October 17, 1994, 62–70.
3. Sherry Lehman and Micki Brook, *It Was Better in the Backseat: How to Recharge Your Sex Life* (Holbrook, Mass.: Bob Adams, Inc., 1994), 129.

4. Peter Nelson, "Will Marriage Change Your Sex Life?" *Glamour,* May 1994, 224–225.
5. Laura Guerrero and Peter A. Anderson, "Patterns of Matching and Initiation: Touch Behavior and Touch Avoidance Across Romantic Relationship Stages," *Journal of Nonverbal Behavior,* 18, no. 2 (1994): 137–53.
6. Pepper Schwartz, Ph.D., "Modernizing Marriage," *Psychology Today,* September/October 1994, 86.
7. Curtis Pesmen, "Stage Fright," *Men's Fitness,* March 1994, 37, 39.

Chapter 7

1. Julie Bennett, "A Labor Union," *Chicago Tribune,* April 26, 1994, sec. 6, 1.
2. Susan Forward, Ph.D., *Money Demons: Keep Them from Sabotaging Your Relationships—and Your Life* (New York: Bantam, 1994), 10–11.

Chapter 8

1. Cranor Graves, *Building a Marriage* (Hyperion, 1993), 13.
2. Clifford Notarius, Ph.D., and Howard Markman, Ph.D., *We Can Work it Out* (New York: G. P. Putnam's Sons, 1993), 139–43.
3. Barry Dym and Michael Glenn, "Forecast for Couples—Conflict?" *Psychology Today,* July 1993, 78.

Chapter 9

1. Helen E. Fisher, *Anatomy of Love: The Natural History of Monogamy, Adultery and Divorce* (New York: W. W. Norton and Co., 1992), 65.
2. Stephen L. Corson, M.D., *Conquering Infertility: A Guide for Couples* (New York: Prentice-Hall, 1991), 6. Dorling Kindersly Limited and the AMA, *The American Medical Association Encyclopedia of Medicine* (New York: Random House, 1989), 586.
3. Beth Livermore, "Why Women's Orgasms Matter," *Self,* February, 1994, 56.

Chapter 10

1. Jean Sherman, "Boy Friends," *BRIDE'S,* April/May 1990, 150.
2. "Good Advice," *BRIDE'S,* June/July 1993, 162.
3. Elizabeth Birkelund Oberbeck, "Little Black Books: His and Yours," *Married Woman,* February/March 1994, 85.
4. Bryan Brook, *Design Your Love Life: Intimacy with Independence, Commitment without Confinement* (New York: Walker and Co. 1990), 137.
5. Herb Goldberg, Ph.D., *What Men Really Want* (New York: Signet/Penguin Books, 1991), 137–38.
6. Harriet Webster, "Friendshifts After Marriage," *BRIDE'S,* February/March 1987, 448.
7. Barbara S. Smalley, "The Six Most Common Marriage Myths," *Modern Bride,* February/March 1993, 42.
8. Susan Page, *Now that I'm Married, Why Isn't Everything Perfect?* (New York: Little, Brown, 1994), 96.

Afterword

1. Linda Murray, "The Lone Wolf Syndrome," *Longevity,* November 1994, 34.

Index

About the Author

Curtis Pesmen has been a writer and editor at *Esquire, SPORT,* and *SELF* magazines. His previous books include *How a Man Ages* and *What She Wants: A Man's Guide to Women.* In addition, his articles have appeared in *Glamour, GQ, Ladies Home Journal, Redbook, US,* and other magazines. Currently Features Editor of *SELF,* Pesmen, a newlywed, lives with his wife in New York City.